Fra Angelico

San Marco, Florence

Fra Angelico

San Marco, Florence

William Hood

GEORGE BRAZILLER   NEW YORK

Published in 1995 by George Braziller, Inc.
Text copyright ©1995 George Braziller, Inc.
Illustrations (except for Figures 2 & 22) courtesy of Nicolò Orsi Battaglini
Figures 2 & 22: Drawings by Timothy Koehle; photographs courtesy of the author

For information, please address the publisher:
George Braziller, Inc.
60 Madison Avenue
New York, New York 10010

LIBRARY OF CONGRESS CATALOGING-IN-PUBLICATION DATA:
Hood, William, 1940-
    Fra Angelico : San Marco, Florence / William Hood.
      p.   cm. — (The Great Fresco Cycles of the Renaissance)
    Includes bibliographical references.
    ISBN 0-8076-1393-2
1. Angelico, Fra, ca. 1400-1455—Criticism and interpretation.
2. Jesus Christ—Art.   3. Spirituality in art. 4. San Marco
(Monastery : Florence, Italy)
I. Angelico, Fra, ca. 1400-1455. II. Title. III. Series.
ND623.F5H67   1995   95-17651
759.5—dc20   CIP

Opposite title page: Aerial View of San Marco, Florence

Designed by Abby Goldstein

Printed by A.G.M., Arese, Italy

CONTENTS

I dedicate this book to John Powers Adams and Francis Xavier Walter
To celebrate the fortieth year of our friendship.

ECCE QUAM BONUM

ACKNOWLEDGMENTS

*T*he joys of friendship have graced my Fra Angelico studies since I began them almost thirteen years ago, and this little book is no exception. Friends and colleagues who are authors of other titles in this series kindly shared their advice and encouragement: Andrew Ladis, Charles Dempsey, and Jonathan Riess. Oberlin College's generous grant of Research Status Appointment for 1994-95 meant that I was free to respond when Adrienne Baxter, my editor at George Braziller, Inc., kindly invited me to write the book and then supported the project with invariable courtesy and efficiency. My chief debt is to my friends Lynn Adams, Faye Walter, and Timothy Whitsel for reading a draft of the Introduction. Their comments and suggestions—to support a syntactical change, one of them wrote, "I don't like it and I am an *average* reader!"—straightened out the prose every time it started to twist and turn in the convoluted locutions (a fellow student once accused me of writing in transliterated German) to which this art historian is so liable.

INTRODUCTION

I. San Marco as a Place

Sight-seeing in Florence can be hard work. Whatever the weather, window-shoppers drift over the Ponte Vecchio in untidy schools and float into the narrow streets like stunned fish. Disheveled students, mostly Americans waiting to call home for money, loiter in the arcade at the entrance to the post office in the Piazza della Repubblica; inside, confused foreigners shuttle from one indifferent clerk to another in the pursuit of postage stamps. Dazed museum-goers form never-moving lines outside the Uffizi and the Accademia, and even those intrepid souls who do gain entrance need to be tall just to see above the heads of other art lovers.

How to escape? Find a cloister. These square or rectangular outdoor rooms are everywhere—one lies alongside any major monastic church—and they offer tranquil retreats for foot-sore sightseers. They were designed for lay visitors like today's tourists, as well as for the resident community of monks, nuns, or friars. The public entrance always led directly to the major cloister where community members met with outsiders. Guests were frequently invited to see the important common rooms—the meeting or chapter room, the dining room or refectory, and so forth—that opened off this outer cloister, and these spaces were often decorated with handsome paintings or sculptures. Tucked away among the monastic buildings were other cloisters, reserved exclusively for the religious who lived there, where complete silence was the unvarying rule. But in the first cloister some conversation was and still is expected, although one soon discovers that fellow visitors tend to lower their voices.

The cloister of San Marco looks today much as it did in the fifteenth century (fig. 1). It is a white stucco cube, open to the sky. On all four sides, arches spring from columns of the traditional Florentine gray stone, called, appropriately enough, *pietra serena* ("serene stone"). The glossy terra-cotta floor under the ambulatory vaults even looks cool; low parapets surround the green carpet of grass in the center, inviting visitors to sit for a while in the shade of stately cypress trees.

The cloister leads to the other parts of San Marco now open to the public. These form the original priory, comprised of the chapter

Figure 1: Florence, Cloister of San Marco, general view

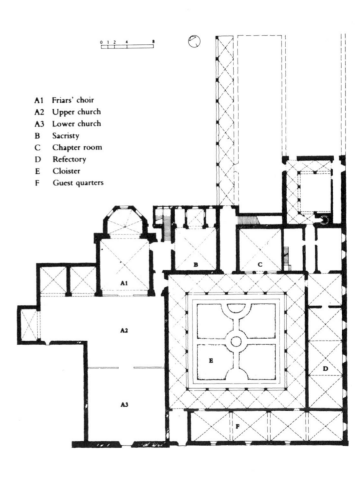

A1 Friars' choir
A2 Upper church
A3 Lower church
B   Sacristy
C   Chapter room
D   Refectory
E   Cloister
F   Guest quarters

Figure 2: Florence, San Marco, reconstructed plan of 1450, ground floor

room, the refectory, the guest quarters, and on the second floor, the dormitory and library (fig. 2). The rest of the building grew organically out of this original fabric as more and more men became friars. San Marco remains a Dominican community to this day. The friars, who occupy the large second cloister reached through the passageway alongside the chapter room, serve the adjoining parish church. Just as during the Renaissance, San Marco is a center of Florentine religious life.

In the Renaissance, it was also home to two great painters, Fra Angelico (c. 1400–1455) and Fra Bartolommeo (1472–1517). Today the refectory houses paintings by Fra Bartolommeo and other artists of his generation, while the old guest quarters, found along the cloister's entrance side, is now a long gallery filled with Fra Angelico's panel paintings.

The most remarkable legacy of Renaissance art at San Marco, however, is its treasure of fresco paintings. Between about 1440 and about 1452, Fra Angelico and his assistants covered the entire complex with more than fifty of them.[1] They adorn the walls of the cloister itself, the chapter room, and before it was enlarged in the sixteenth century, the refectory; upstairs there are three frescoes in the corridors and one in each of the forty-four cells. Even while resting in the cloister's peaceful setting, one may contemplate Fra Angelico's huge image of *Saint Dominic with the Crucifix* (see Pl. 1) opposite the entrance or the great *Crucifixion* (see Pl. 4) in the chapter room. They convey a refreshing, fifteenth-century sense of the beauty of holiness that the Dominicans of San Marco found in their everyday lives.

Although Fra Angelico adapted the subjects and even his style to suit the particular function of each fresco within its appointed space, he also designed the whole ensemble to keep the ancient ideals and traditions of the Dominican order fresh in the friars' minds. Therefore, when modern beholders meditate on these frescoes with their original meanings and functions in mind, their imaginations can travel far beyond the noisy distractions of the world outside the cloister. This book is designed as a companion on that journey and as a guide for contemplating Fra Angelico's art as a monument of Dominican culture in Renaissance Florence.

San Marco's History

What we know about San Marco comes primarily from two Dominican sources, the chronicles of San Marco and San Domenico in Fiesole. Chronicles are the routine records maintained by religious communities. They itemize things such as newcomers to the order; the names and numbers of professions, ordinations, and deaths; and other notable events such as benefactions and natural disasters. The chronicle of San Marco is especially rich for the first twenty years of the community's life in Florence, which began in

1436. It and the less lengthy chronicle of San Domenico in Fiesole, San Marco's parent community, supplemented by a remarkably small number of reliable documents, tell the following tale.[2]

The Observant Dominicans at San Domenico, Fiesole

In October 1435 the Dominicans at San Domenico dedicated their newly constructed church and convent, which had been built to accommodate twenty friars, on the steep road leading north to the ancient Etruscan hill town of Fiesole, whose majestic view across Florence and the Arno Valley into the hills of the Chianti region charms sightseers to this day (fig. 3). It was a convent of Observant, or reformed, friars. Toward the end of the fourteenth century, a vocal minority within the Order of Preachers, which is the Dominicans' official name, persuaded the majority that the order had grown into habits of living that fell far short of what Saint Dominic had envisioned when he founded it in the early thirteenth century. In response, by 1400 the Dominicans had established a few Italian and German convents for these friars, where they were free to observe (hence the appellation Observant) the primitive customs in all their

Figure 3: View of San Domenico in Fiesole

rigor. Among other voluntary hardships, this meant rising at about two o'clock in the morning to sing the Night Office; gathering every few hours in the church for more prayers; eating a vegetarian diet of only one full meal a day; keeping complete silence in the conventual buildings, and engaging in other ascetic practices that the early Dominicans had adopted from Cistercian monks. Most of all, like the parallel Observance in the Order of Friars Minor, or Franciscans, the Observant Dominicans forswore all possessions that would guarantee a reliable income.

Since the earliest days of Christian monasticism, monks and nuns had surrendered their rights to own private property. But gifts of land, securities, and other unmovable goods bestowed on them by popes, kings, and nobles turned many religious institutions into rich corporations. The chief beneficiaries, of course, were their members, and individual poverty was therefore hardly a difficulty for residents of a monastery that maintained its members in comfort. The wealth of the religious orders was, in fact, one of the main complaints leveled against the institutional church by both clergy and laypeople in the High Middle Ages. Saint Dominic and Saint Francis of Assisi were contemporaries. Saint Dominic died in 1221, Saint Francis in 1226, and the two men concurred with the general perception that church authorities had grown unconscionably rich at the expense of the poor and, what was more, that wealth had corrupted the church's soul as well as its body.

To protect their followers from the deleterious effects of wealth, and to bear a witness of identity with the poor, Saints Francis and Dominic forbade their followers from accepting gifts of land, rental property, or securities from even the most well meaning benefactors. The founders believed that, like the poor, Dominican and Franciscan friars should be beggars—mendicants—and to that end each of them introduced the rule of institutional poverty into his order of friars. Sometimes this meant that the friars literally went from house to house asking for food. More commonly it required the superiors of these communities to be skillful—and full-time—fund-raisers. Unlike their counterparts in modern charitable organizations, however, Dominican priors and Franciscan guardians, as the superiors were called, could never seek to increase the endowment. On the contrary, everything they collected went into the general operating budget, which was almost always encumbered, never quite adequate, and systemically incapable of supporting capital planning. And that is exactly what Saints Francis and Dominic intended.

Each founder encountered great resistance to the notion of institutional poverty even within his own order. Supported by popes and other dignitaries who did not wish to suffer by comparison with the mendicants, both the Franciscans and the Dominicans had abandoned the principle of institutional poverty within a generation following the founders' deaths.

Institutional poverty had been the most revolutionary and controversial aspect of religious life introduced into the church at large by the mendicants. Not surprisingly, when the Observants of both orders pushed to reinstate the practice around 1400, they found strong opposition from the large majority of friars who wanted things to stay as they were. For that and other reasons, Franciscan and Dominican Observant communities tended to be composed of small groups of exceptionally zealous members and to establish themselves in towns or on the peripheries of large cities, where living was cheaper and where they would not compete with the huge houses of conventual mendicants that characterized every city in Europe by the close of the Middle Ages. That is why the convent of Observant Dominicans was in Fiesole rather than in Florence. San Domenico was, and to this day remains, a tiny community, seldom exceeding the minimum membership necessary for a Dominican community to maintain its status as a priory, that is, twelve professed friars in addition to a smaller number of novices and lay brothers.

The Foundation of San Marco in Florence

In January 1436, three months after the dedication of San Domenico, the Dominicans sent a contingent of nine friars from Fiesole to take over the ancient Silvestrine monastery of San Marco in the center of Florence (fig. 4). It stands along the north side of the piazza at the end of the wide street (Via Larga), now Via Cavour, that leads north from the Cathedral of Santa Maria del Fiore and the Baptistery of Saint John (fig. 5). In light of what we know about the Observance, and especially about its adherence to institutional poverty, this move seems remarkable.

It was. Taking over San Marco can only have signified that the Observants had achieved a particularly favorable consensus of both ecclesiastical and political officials. Pope Eugenius IV (papacy 1431–47) was living in Florence at that time. A strong supporter of reform, he personally ordered the Silvestrine monks to vacate the property on the charges, perhaps trumped up, that they were living "without a good reputation" and "with neither poverty nor chastity."

Furthermore, behind the public surface of these events was a long series of maneuvers whereby the Dominicans had successfully enlisted the aid of the two richest and most powerful citizens of Florence, the brothers Cosimo and Lorenzo de' Medici. At exactly this moment, under Cosimo's leadership the Medici were beginning their long ascendancy over Florentine life, which lasted, with one notable interruption in the 1490s, until the family died out in the eighteenth century. Beginning in the 1530s, the descendants of the Medici ruled Florence as grand dukes and allied themselves by marriage with the major royal families of Europe. Although in 1436

Figure 4: Chain map of Florence

Figure 5: View of San Marco from the piazza

these developments lay in the future, Cosimo's support of important religious institutions, like San Marco, was one of the major foundation stones on which his dynasty was to rest. The Medici house, in fact, stood just a few hundred feet from San Marco on the Via Larga, and their parish church of San Lorenzo was only a few blocks away.

Just as effective politicians operate out of strongly organized neighborhood wards in today's large cities, so in Renaissance Florence local political power depended on a single family's firm control of its neighbors and the surrounding business establishments. San Marco was in the Medici neighborhood. Under the cooperative Dominicans it became a symbol of Medici leadership in the city from the time of its founding in 1436 right through the rest of the fifteenth century. Cosimo's grandson, Lorenzo the Magnificent, quarreled bitterly with Fra Girolamo Savonarola, the charismatic prior of San Marco whom many regarded as a crazed fanatic. Yet just before his death in April 1492, Lorenzo de' Medici begged for Savonarola's blessing. With a gesture that showed once and for all how the balance of power had shifted, Savonarola refused.

In Cosimo de' Medici, therefore, the Dominicans at San Marco had found the perfect patron for an Observant foundation. With Cosimo's unfailing financial support, they were able to have the Florentine architect and sculptor Michelozzo remodel the church and rebuild the conventual buildings, which had fallen into bad repair. It

Figure 6: Benozzo Gozzoli, *Procession of the Magi,* Palazzo Medici-Riccardi, Florence

was into these new spaces that Fra Angelico moved with a team of painters some time around 1440, with Cosimo's full financial backing. Cosimo also gave San Marco its magnificent garden and, most important, the enormous library of precious manuscripts and incunabula that made it the first public library of modern times.

The deep religious and political ties connecting San Marco with the Medici are perhaps best illustrated by a simple observation. On the walls of the chapel in the family's palace, Benozzo Gozzoli frescoed a great *Procession of the Magi,* which shows male members of the Medici family riding in triumph with the Three Wise Men on their way to Bethlehem (fig. 6). Not fifty feet from that spot, in the street below, Florence's own annual Magi Procession, subsidized by the Medici, moved from the cathedral to San Marco, which for generations before the Dominicans moved there had been the goal of the yearly parade. Benozzo's painting, therefore, records political realities in the shape of religious myth, just as the political myth of the Florentine Magi Procession centered on what were believed to be religious realities.

II. Fra Angelico's Life and Career

*T*he first lengthy record of Fra Angelico's life comes to us in the same book in which the lives of many other Renaissance artists were first portrayed, in Giorgio Vasari's *Lives of the Artists*, published first in 1550 and again, in a much enlarged edition, in 1568.[3] Vasari was a highly successful painter and architect in his own right and passionately devoted to his profession and its history. He was also sensitive to the gaps in his knowledge, and when possible, he sought out eyewitnesses who could add or confirm information for his biographies of Italian artists.

Vasari acquired most of his knowledge about Fra Angelico from a friar at San Marco named Fra Eustachio, at that time an old man much famed for his prodigious memory. Born in 1473, at twenty-four Fra Eustachio had become a lay brother at San Marco under Savonarola; as Fra Angelico himself had died in 1455, we may assume that Fra Eustachio actually knew people who had known Fra Angelico. In interviewing Fra Eustachio, then, Vasari was as close to an eyewitness as he could get. What's more, by profession Fra Eustachio was a manuscript illuminator, and he prided himself as continuing a tradition said to have been begun by Fra Angelico and his natural brother, Fra Benedetto, a scribe who was also a Dominican friar.

Even though Fra Angelico had been dead for the better part of a century by the time Vasari talked with Fra Eustachio, the artist's legend at San Marco was still very much alive. Fra Eustachio did not tell Vasari very much about Fra Angelico's frescoes, and Vasari himself never saw the paintings in the dormitory, because in his day they were restricted to the view of the Dominican friars. But Vasari reported what he heard, and he heard a very great deal about Fra Angelico's character. It was Fra Angelico's character, not his paintings, that interested Fra Eustachio.

Vasari's Life *of Fra Angelico*

It is because of Vasari that subsequent generations, including ours, have always thought of the artist as uncommonly pious. Thus, it is probably Fra Eustachio speaking through Vasari when the *Lives* say that Fra Angelico never picked up a brush without praying first, that he always wept while painting crucifixes, and that he never made corrections because he believed that the first brushstrokes revealed God's will. Although it is hard to know whether things like these are really true, it is entirely plausible that Fra Angelico really did, as Vasari says, refuse a dish of meat because he had not received permission from his prior, even though the pope himself had offered it. Less certain is the story that the pope also offered Fra Angelico the archbishopric of Florence, which the painter declined out of modesty but nominated the successful candidate, the prior of San Marco, Fra Antonino Pierozzi, in his own stead. At any rate, as the Italians say, "Se non è vero è ben trovato," which means something like, "[Even] if it's not true, it makes a good story."

Obviously, this is the stuff of hagiography and not art history. In other words, what Fra Eustachio told Vasari, and Vasari passed on to his readers, was likely a myth about the artist invented in the fifteenth century for the Dominicans' own propagandistic purposes. Affectionate if not-quite-accurate stories like these began to emerge almost immediately after the artist's death in 1455. Thus it should come as no surprise to learn that sorting fact from fiction has been a major task of Fra Angelico scholars. Over the past forty years their labors in the archives have assembled the evidence for the following account of the artist's life.[4]

A Documentary Life of Fra Angelico

Fra Angelico began life as Guido di Piero. He was born in the Mugello, a broad alluvial valley, rich in farmland, north of Florence just beyond the hill towns of Fiesole and Settignano. Most of the Medici estates were in the Mugello, and Borgo San Lorenzo, the main town, bears the name of a saint who was a popular patron for male Medici family members.

Fra Angelico's father, Piero, may have been a prosperous farmer. That he was at least more than solvent seems certain. One of his daughters married a Florentine property owner, which would have required a substantial dowry. Learning to read cost money, too, and it seems likely that Piero was able to provide his children with a rudimentary education as well as make it possible for two of his sons to move to Florence, where they were trained in lucrative professions. One of the sons became a manuscript illuminator and the other a scribe. This, in turn, suggests that they had at least one older brother who would have stayed in the Mugello and carried on their father's trade, whatever that was.

The brothers were named Guido and Benedetto, but we do not know when either of them was born. Tradition has it that Benedetto was the elder, and circumstances make it all but certain that Guido was born in the late 1390s, perhaps as late as 1400. Benedetto became the scribe, Guido the painter. Both became Dominican friars. Guido di Piero took the religious name Fra Giovanni da Fiesole, and since the sixteenth century at the latest Fra Giovanni da Fiesole has carried the fond nickname of Fra Angelico.

At the turn of the fifteenth century, Florence was a major European center for the production of illustrated manuscripts of superb quality. The hub of this industry was the Camaldolese monastery of

Santa Maria degli Angeli, in the heart of Florence. Although the majority of scriptoria were headed and staffed by laymen, they were all located close to the Angeli in the neighborhood around the parish church of San Michele Visdomini, where the two sons of Piero lived, practically in the shadow of Florence cathedral.

The brothers must have moved to Florence about 1415. At that time, the dominant figure in the Angeli scriptorium, indeed the dominant figure in all of Florentine painting whether miniature or monumental, was the Camaldolese monk known as Don Lorenzo Monaco. Many scholars have thought that Lorenzo Monaco was Guido's teacher, but one of the major problems with understanding Fra Angelico's beginnings is the apparent loss of all documented work from this early period, although art historians are always hopeful that some day a painting known only through the documents will turn up.[5] Occasionally, that happens.

Although Don Lorenzo Monaco may or may not have been Fra Angelico's actual teacher, it was certainly within the broad parameters of his painting style that Fra Angelico's hand was trained. Whether the tiniest miniatures or the biggest altarpieces and frescoes, Fra Angelico's art inspires the use of adjectives like *gorgeous, sumptuous, elegant.*

Fra Angelico's Training

A brief look at a miniature and a panel painting will lay the foundations of Lorenzo Monaco's approach to the art of painting. Between 1385 and 1397 the scriptorium at Santa Maria degli Angeli produced a twelve-volume antiphonary for the use of the monks' choir. Each of the large volumes is lavishly illuminated, and of those miniatures by Lorenzo Monaco himself we may study a historiated initial (fig. 7).[6]

The initial's effect is rather like looking at and then through a trellis. At the inner contours the letter's basic shape is clearly discernible, but a whole garden of plant shapes sprouts from the outer edges and wriggles across the sheet like a rambling rose in June. Inside the initial's loop, Lorenzo Monaco showed a partial view of Christ's tomb. Typical for the period, it is a kind of sarcophagus resting on the ground, the lid knocked off to the side, and behind it is a view of mountains. In this configuration the letter becomes a window frame because it actually blocks out part of the scene, and because one looks through and not just at it, the initial belongs to the *visual* as well as the verbal message that the miniature sends. An angel sits on the sarcophagus's edge, facing the Three Marys, who, like the sleeping soldiers, are only partially visible. Clearly, then, Lorenzo Monaco decided to provide more information than the text alone does, and the clattering jumble of forms provides a visual analogue to the stupendous miracle of the Resurrection itself. Notice, for example, how the crossbar of the *A* counters the sharp corner of the sarcophagus lid, which the hilltops in the left distance echo. The craftsmanship is exquisite, the sumptuous materials like gold and ultramarine blue are prodigal, and the scintillating colors, together with the springing rhythms of the forms, give this little work of art a psychological power far greater than its actual size.

Just so, the initial *R* on folio 33 of the famous manuscript numbered 558, made for San Marco in the early 1430s by the shop at

Figure 7: Lorenzo Monaco, Three Marys at the Tomb in an Initial A. Paris, Musée du Louvre, Cabinet des Dessins (RF 830)

Fiesole and still at San Marco, shows that Fra Angelico reached the summit of his achievements in manuscript illumination by following Lorenzo Monaco as a guide (fig. 8).[7] Fleshy tendrils of blue and red wrap around the letter like tenacious vines, and the letter itself, as in the Camaldolese manuscript just discussed, is both field and

Figure 8: Fra Angelico, The Annunciation in an Initial R. Museo di San Marco, Florence (Cod. 558, fol. 33v)

frame for the little representation of the Annunciation that pictorially marks the feast to whose music the chant on this page belongs. The Virgin sits in the lower part and looks up at the angel Gabriel hovering outside. Notice how neatly Fra Angelico designed each figure to fit, as though naturally, into the initial's abstract contours. Above, a foreshortened figure of God the Father reaches "out" of a deep blue space and sends the dove of the Holy Spirit soaring "down" to the Virgin "in front of" the letter itself.

Figure 10: Fra Angelico, *Virgin and Child and Saints* and *Stories of Saint Peter Martyr,* Museo di San Marco, Florence

Figure 9: Fra Angelico, The Assassination of Saint Peter Martyr in an Initial P. Museo di San Marco, Florence (Cod. 558, fol. 41v)

Figure 11: Fra Angelico, *Martyrdom of Saint Peter Martyr,* detail from Figure 10 (above)

Likewise, the letter *P* telescopes onto the scene of Saint Peter Martyr's assassination painted in the loop and cropped all around like Lorenzo Monaco's scene of the Three Marys, its landscape and narrative energy no less developed than the Camaldolese model (fig. 9).[8] These illuminations show that Fra Angelico could rival and even surpass Lorenzo Monaco.

Fra Angelico's Early Works

Paintings such as an altarpiece made in the 1420s for the Observant Dominican nuns at San Pier Martire in Florence show two, somehow mutually exclusive, aspects of Fra Angelico's mind (fig. 10). On the one hand, the little scene of the Assassination of Saint Peter Martyr is nearly identical to the manuscript version just discussed; indeed, they were painted at about the same time (fig. 11). In the central panel and the corresponding section in the altarpiece for San Domenico in Fiesole of about 1425, Fra Angelico's long, fluid figures with their curving, elastic gestures and sinuous torrents of shimmering stuffs swirling in eddies around the Virgin's feet tell of his studied reflections on Lorenzo Monaco's art (figs. 12, 13).[9] On the other hand, the differences between Fra Angelico and Lorenzo Monaco are more interesting than the similarities. They reveal that Fra Angelico was far from an imitator, that he was independent minded and committed to aesthetic propositions that Lorenzo Monaco never really entertained.

These aesthetic propositions rested on the tacit assumption that the task of art was the imitation of nature, more or less as it appears to our eyes. The idea was not original with Fra Angelico, and he was by no means unique in his endeavors. The common interest of Florentine painters in the representation of space, for example, was to lead to the development of vanishing-point perspective. And artists' concern with the natural weight of the human body led them to researches into antique sculpture completely unprecedented in

Figure 12: Fra Angelico, *Virgin and Child and Saints*. San Domenico, Fiesole

European art before the second quarter of the fifteenth century. Fra Angelico's experiments visible in these two paintings, in other words, put him in the company of artists like Gentile da Fabriano and Masaccio, of Ghiberti and Brunelleschi and Donatello. Indeed, there are close harmonies with these masters to be found in Fra Angelico's work of the 1420s and 1430s.

What is remarkable, among other things, is the fact that, as a Dominican friar, nothing constrained him to keep abreast. He was not in competition, and he never sought the sorts of commissions, as the other artists just mentioned did, that would put him in the limelight. He was remarkably single-minded as a painter, and this feature of his character and intellect is doubtless related to his other vocation, which was that of a Dominican friar.

Fra Angelico's Conversion

Although Guido di Piero's beginnings as a painter may be uncertain, of his personal piety there can be no doubt. In 1418 he joined a confraternity, a kind of religious club, that met at the church of Santa Maria del Carmine, where Masaccio and Masolino were to work in the Brancacci Chapel in the 1420s. Dedicated to Saint

Figure 13: Lorenzo Monaco, *Madonna of Humility*. The Brooklyn Museum Collection, New York

Nicholas, this confraternity counted large numbers of Florentine laypeople among its members, who regularly gathered to pray and to listen to sermons. At some point, most likely around 1421, Guido decided to follow his pious instincts to their limit and to assume the habit of a Dominican friar. His brother Benedetto did likewise. By this time Guido was at least twenty-one years old, probably closer to twenty-five, and it is worth considering both his decision and the age at which he reached it in the context of Florentine religious life in that period.

For the four years between 1419 and 1423, that is, at exactly the period during which the young painter decided to become a Dominican friar, Florence was host to Fra Manfredi da Vercelli, a famous Dominican preacher.[10] Preaching was a popular form of entertainment in those days—sermons could go on for better than three hours and audiences could reach as many as ten thousand people—and Dominicans were specially skilled at it. Saint Dominic, after all, had founded his order specifically for *preachers*. Fra Manfredi's message, designed to appeal to laypeople, to ordinary men and women, urged them to adopt lives whose simplicity and devotion would set them apart from their more worldly neighbors, among whom, however, they would continue to live.

Christians of this period formed strong emotional bonds with holy persons, especially with Christ and the Virgin Mary; they maintained these allegiances through vividly imagined meditations on the events of the saints' lives. These meditations and the prayers that accompanied them were found in so-called books of hours, the religious texts made in response to the growing literacy among the middle and upper classes. Like the sermons of popular preachers such as Fra Manfredi, books of hours underscored the intensely subjective relationship that the devout soul was encouraged to develop with God. Manuscripts of this kind—there were no printed books yet—were among the most common products of scriptoria such as the one where Fra Angelico worked. We may suppose that he was familiar with their contents and perhaps even owned a modest copy himself.

This form of intense, introverted spirituality is usually called the *Devotio Moderna*, or Modern Devotion. It spread all over Europe and gave rise to new forms of pious living in the fourteenth century, especially in the decades after the devastations of the Black Death, or bubonic plague, in 1347–51. Communities of laypeople who owned property in common, lived together, and devoted themselves to the service of others sprang up in northern Europe. Known as Beguines (women) and Begards (men), these groups became important forces in the religious culture that prepared the way for the Reformation. Although the movement never came to much south of the Alps, in Italy the Observant reforms of the major religious orders, especially the Dominicans and Franciscans, attracted like-minded souls to their numbers.

As Fra Manfredi was himself an Observant, not conventual, Dominican, we may assume that he passed his Florentine years in the Observant community at San Domenico in Fiesole rather than among the conventual friars at Santa Maria Novella in Florence itself. It, therefore, seems probable that the painter Guido di Piero, having already found himself attracted to the strong religiosity of the Confraternity of Saint Nicholas at Santa Maria del Carmine, was drawn into the Dominican orbit at Fiesole through the preaching of Fra Manfredi. What is certain and not just probable is that by 1423 the documents no longer refer to him as "Guido di Piero." Thenceforward, he was known as "frate Giovanni de' frati di san Domenicho da fiesole," "Friar John of the Friars of Saint Dominic in Fiesole." And it was as Fra Giovanni, not as Guido di Piero, that Fra Angelico entered the history of art.

It is easy enough to appreciate what the brothers Guido and Benedetto di Piero gave up when they took the Dominican habit. The vows of poverty, chastity, and obedience meant that they surrendered their right to own private property, to marry and have children, and to make personal and professional decisions on the basis of their own best interests rather than on the will of an elected official. For most people, then as now, these are obvious and even insupportable disciplines. But were there advantages as well? Apart from membership in the Order of Preachers, which meant that they moved into one of the elite sections of late-medieval society, the brothers also guaranteed themselves a degree of professional freedom that no artisan in the lay state could have enjoyed.

The Friar/Painter

For Fra Angelico, as I shall call him henceforth, becoming a Dominican put him at a significant professional advantage. First and most obvious is the fact that he no longer had to worry about earning a living; the Dominican order saw to the friars' practical needs. Not only did it provide food and shelter, but friars, whether scholars or artisans, had places to work and tools to work with. Beyond that, of course, Fra Angelico's clerical state meant that he was free from the economic competition that plagued any master of any craft. Indeed, it seems that as soon as he had completed the year-long novitiate about 1423, he was already at work on commissions for his own community. Throughout the 1420s and well into the next decade, in fact, there was no dearth of work. A large number of commissions from other Observant communities, as well as from the conventual house at Santa Maria Novella in Florence, augmented the modest but steady assignments from well-to-do Florentine burghers. This is not to say that Fra Angelico was freed from the necessity to work. To the contrary. He and Fra Benedetto, as his brother continued to be known, established a workshop at San Domenico, which produced manuscripts, panel paintings in all sizes, and, of course, large-scale frescoes. The shop stayed so busy during the brothers' life-times—Fra Benedetto died in 1448 and Fra Angelico, as we have seen, in 1455—that some of their collaborators, such as Zanobi Strozzi, actually moved from Florence to Fiesole in order to be close to work.[11] There is every reason to believe, in fact, that the studio at San Domenico was the community's major source of income for several decades. Unlike the Observants at San Marco, the friars at San Domenico had no Cosimo de' Medici.

In the early 1430s, Fra Angelico's reputation caught the attention of clients bearing the grandest names in Florentine society, Medici and Strozzi. Furthermore, he won an extremely lucrative commission from the Guild of Linen Merchants, and this placed him squarely in the forefront of Florentine artists (fig. 14). Throughout the 1430s and halfway through the next decade, in fact, it could be said that Fra Angelico was the most prominent painter in Florence, even though he continued to work almost, but not quite, exclusively for Dominican clients.

Fra Angelico reached the pinnacle of professional artistic success in 1445. In that year Pope Eugenius IV, who had seen his work at San Marco, called him to Rome. Eugenius's successor, Pope Nicholas V (papacy 1447–55), employed Fra Angelico as well. Over the next ten years Fra Angelico painted at least two papal chapels in the Vatican Palace and, perhaps, frescoes in Old Saint Peter's Basilica (fig. 15). Tragically, with the exception of the Chapel of Nicholas V, which

Figure 14: Fra Angelico, Linaiuoli tabernacle. Museo di San Marco, Florence

one may still visit just outside Raphael's *stanze*, all of Fra Angelico's monumental Roman paintings were destroyed in the sixteenth century. The present Saint Peter's began to rise in 1506, making it necessary to raze the fourth-century Constantinian basilica piecemeal. Along with it, of course, went all its wall paintings. Pope Paul III (papacy 1534–49) tore down one of Fra Angelico's chapels in the Vatican Palace when he built a monumental staircase called the Scala Reggia in the 1530s. And a group of enormous frescoes at Santa Maria sopra Minerva, the Dominican convent in Rome, disappeared when its cloister was razed in the eighteenth century.

These are terrible losses to the body of Renaissance monumental painting, of course, but they are particularly sad for Fra Angelico's work. That is because the road to fame as a painter in Renaissance Rome and Florence went through one and only one landscape, that of large-scale mural painting, and that means fresco. As it happens, therefore, the only surviving frescoes by Fra Angelico are the paintings in the Chapel of Nicholas V in Rome and the complex for San Marco in Florence. Because so few of Fra Angelico's frescoes survive, those at San Marco are all the more important for the history of Florentine painting.

Not only did Fra Angelico make wonderful paintings in all media and on every scale from the tiny to the huge, he ran a large workshop that turned out work of very high technical and aesthetic quality, all at a very brisk clip. He also enjoyed the Dominicans'

Figure 15: Fra Angelico, Chapel of Nicholas V, the Vatican

confidence, serving in all the important elected posts at his home convent in Fiesole. Unlike Fra Benedetto, who was subprior at San Marco, Fra Angelico never seems to have given up residence at San Domenico, even while the two convents were juridically united during the first nine years of San Marco's life as a Dominican house, from 1436 to 1445.

It happened, though, that Fra Angelico did not die at home in Fiesole, but in Rome. He is buried under the pavement at Santa Maria sopra Minerva, and his elegant Latin epitaph was clearly composed by a friar of much greater learning and sophistication than the down-to-earth artisans who made up Fra Angelico's own community. This author wove traditional Christian sympathies reflected in a paraphrase of Psalm 115 ("Non nobis Domine sed nomine tuam sit gloria," "Not to us, O Lord, but to your name be the glory") into an epitaph characteristic of fifteenth-century humanists who enjoyed reviving the lofty diction of classical antiquity for public inscriptions. Thus, it uses the ancient Latin term for Tuscany (*Etruria*) and includes a sophisticated reference to Apelles, the famous Greek court painter of Alexander the Great. It reads as follows:[12]

NON MIHI SIT LAUDI, QUOD ERAM VELUT ALTER APELLES,
SED QUOD LUCRA TUIS OMNIA, CHRISTE, DABAM:
ALTERA NAM TERRIS OPERA EXTANT, ALTERA CAELO.
URBS ME JOANNEM FLOS TULIT ETRURIAE.
HIC JACET VEN. PICTOR FR. IO. DE FLOR. ORD. PDICATO. ILLV.

M

CCCC

L

V

[Let not me be praised because I was another Apelles,
But because I rendered all my wealth to {what is(?)} yours,
O Christ:
Some {of my} works remain on earth, others in heaven.
The city which is the flower of Tuscany bore me.
Here lies the venerable painter Fra Giovanni of Florence of the illustrious Order of Preachers

1

4

5

5]

Obviously, by the time of Fra Angelico's burial, the Dominicans had already decided to claim a place for him in the annals of history. With his death, his myth was born.

III. The Frescoes of San Marco

*L*ooking at frescoes can be like stepping into a time capsule, because the viewer is standing in exactly the spot where the artist stood while he was working.[13] Because most of the paintings at San Marco were made to be seen up close, it is easy to follow the direction of Fra Angelico's mind by retracing the passage of his hand across the frescoes' surfaces. In the right frame of mind, it is even possible to conjure the soft whoosh of his white woolen habit coming from somewhere just out of sight, because not even long and deep familiarity erases the uncanny sense that there are living if invisible presences in the dormitory.

Fantasies about living presences are well within the domain of psychological experiences imagined by Fra Angelico and the friars who helped him plan the decoration at San Marco. For nowhere else do mural paintings respond more exactly to their physical placement, nowhere more than at San Marco did the artist so vividly encode the paintings with his own presence, directing, suggesting, and even telling viewers how to respond. Every painting is site-specific. This is true, moreover, in every way: the paintings' sizes and shapes were fitted to the wall where they are found; their palettes as well as the subjects and the ways that Fra Angelico interpreted those subjects reflect in very particular ways the exact function of each fresco within the overall scheme of the ensemble. Fra Angelico adapted even the painting technique itself to the didactic mission of sacred art.

Just who planned the program of decoration is a moot question. The extent and complexity of the decoration at San Marco is unprecedented in known monastic situations, suggesting that the Dominicans gave Fra Angelico a free hand. There is no reason to suppose that the artist took orders from some other, more authoritative, source. After all, he himself was a respected member of the Order of Preachers, fully versed in its lore and traditions. The frescoes of San Marco represent Fra Angelico's imagination as a planner, his skills as an entrepreneur, and his gifts as a painter. All of those, of course, he brought under the discipline of his overarching commitment to his vocation as a Dominican friar.

Regarding the subjects in the friars' cells, it would probably be a mistake to look for some kind of blueprint or unitary program that would pull all of them together like the pieces of a conceptual jigsaw puzzle. Furthermore, the number of assistants and the arhythmic sequence of work means that the aesthetic quality ranges from the sublime to the banal. With his own, unassisted or almost unassisted, hand, Fra Angelico painted only *Saint Dominic with the Crucifix* in the cloister (see Pl. 1), the *Crucifixion* in the chapter room (see Pl. 4), the *Annunciation* (see Pl. 10) and the *Madonna of the Shadows* (see Pl. 15) in the dormitory corridors, and probably no more than six of the cell frescoes. The rest, however, were carried out under his supervision.

Frescoes on the Ground Floor

Just as one has escaped the clamor of the piazza outside in order to enter San Marco, so the first painting one sees opens onto those serene places where the human spirit dwells constantly in the divine presence. For opposite the entrance is the fresco showing *Saint Dominic with the Crucifix* at the other end of the west range (fig. 16). The painting's dimensions and shape match those of the entrance itself, and—right away—one realizes that Fra Angelico intended one to notice the symmetry. The five other frescoes in the cloister carry more humble but also more straightforward messages, each representing a specific activity that instantiated these supernatural realities in the friars' daily routine.

Fra Angelico painted lunettes over the doors leading from the cloister to adjoining spaces. At the left of *Saint Dominic with the Crucifix* is the entrance to the choir and sacristy, and over it Saint Peter Martyr enjoins the silence not always observed, we have noticed, in the cloister (fig. 17). Over the entrance to the refectory immediately opposite, a half-length figure of Christ rising out of his tomb reminded the friars that their true nourishment was the Bread

Figure 16: Fra Angelico, *Saint Dominic with the Crucifix. Florence, San Marco, cloister*

Figure 17: View of the door to the church and sacristy. Florence, San Marco

of the Eucharist and not of the dining table (fig. 18); over the entrance to the former guest quarters, Fra Angelico showed two friars receiving Christ, who carries a pilgrim's staff (fig. 19). This is a reminder, lifted from Saint Benedict's Rule for monks, that a guest was to be received as though he were Christ Himself. Over another door on the south range, Saint Thomas Aquinas, the thirteenth-century Dominican intellectual giant, holds an open book against his chest (fig. 20). Although the precise function of this door can no longer be determined, it seems likely that it gave access to the original library, as every Dominican convent had a library and Thomas

Figure 18: Fra Angelico, *Man of Sorrows*. Florence, San Marco, cloister

Figure 19: Fra Angelico, *Christ Being Received as a Pilgrim*. Florence, San Marco, cloister

is their natural patron saint. Now on view in the San Marco Museum is the badly weathered lunette showing Saint Dominic with a scourge, or whip used in the discipline of self-flagellation. Until recently this fresco was attached to its original site at the entrance to the chapter room. This subject seems an odd choice because, other than the church itself, the chapter room was the most public space of any monastic complex. The professed friars met there every day, novices came there to be received into the community, and all visiting dignitaries were greeted and most official con-

Figure 20: Fra Angelico, *Saint Thomas Aquinas*. Florence, San Marco, cloister

tacts with the outside world were made in the chapter room. So why did Fra Angelico show Saint Dominic carrying a scourge rather than, for instance, holding the Dominican order's Rule or some other symbol of ecclesial distinction? Because the scourge symbolized the daily self-flagellation that the early Dominicans practiced when they met in the chapter room, a practice long fallen into disuse before the Observants revived it in Fra Angelico's time. In other words, the fresco stamps this Dominican chapter room with a specifically *Observant* identity.

Like all chapter rooms in large and important monastic foundations, the one at San Marco is handsomely decorated with a *Crucifixion* (fig. 21). Several features make this *Crucifixion* unique, however, and those features pertain, not surprisingly, to both the Observant allegiances of the San Marco community and their debt to Cosimo de' Medici, their patron. Running below the whole painting is a band of portraits in roundels, each linked to the other by a vine issuing from the central medallion, which frames the head of Saint Dominic. Each figure connected by the vine, an obvious symbol of the order, represents a prominent Dominican.

In the main field above, however, Saint Dominic appears again, this time kneeling at the proper right of Christ's Cross. Beyond him, stretching all the way to the painting's right edge, is a group of other monastic figures, most of whom are not Dominican at all. They are, instead, founders of the especially rigorous form of monastic life.

Figure 21: Fra Angelico, *Crucifixion*. Florence, San Marco, chapter room

Once again, therefore, the chapter room decoration asserts San Marco's fundamental Dominican identity, but modified in important symbolic ways to set it apart from the majority, or conventual, style of Dominican living and to associate it with those other movements that, like the Observance, sought a rigorous adherence to the ideals of a life consecrated exclusively to God's service.

At the fresco's far left side, by contrast, Fra Angelico showed Saints Cosmas and Damian; to the right stands Saint Lawrence, wearing the deacon's alb and supporting a grill, with which he was martyred; beyond Saint Lawrence, toward the center, kneels Saint

Mark with his gospel open on his left leg. Just as the right side of the painting reflects the ideals of the Dominican Observance, the left side associates the Observant Dominicans of San Marco with the Medici family. Cosmas and Damian were the family's patron saints, as witness Cosimo's own name, because they were physicians, or *medici*. As we have seen, Saint Lawrence was the patron of Borgo San Lorenzo, the major town in the Mugello, which was the Medici's seat of rural power; he was also the patron of the Medici's parish church in Florence; and many Medici men, for example Lorenzo the Magnificent, bore his name. Saint Mark, obviously, is present as the convent's own patron saint.

Two aesthetic features of this fresco, furthermore, underscore just how careful Fra Angelico was to embed every aspect of the paintings with meaning. We have seen that the monastic saints are on the right, the Medici saints on the left. Thus, it is worth noticing that the Medici saints are more important, hierarchically, because they appear on *Christ*'s right, just as do the Good Thief and the biblical figures beneath the Cross. This bit of institutional, even political, submissiveness on Fra Angelico's part is easy to miss. It is also easy to miss the remarkable fact that the only passage of pure ultramarine blue in all of San Marco is to be found on the Virgin's cloak, barely visible as she swoons in grief. Ultramarine is the oldest and most technically specific device whereby a painter and his patron could honor a distinguished personage. That is because ultramarine

was by far the most precious of all the painter's materials. It is beautiful, it is extremely resistant to the damaging effects of light, and it is very rare. Consequently, painters' contracts of the period frequently specified the exact quantity of ultramarine that the patron had authorized the master to use. At San Marco, whose frescoes are distinctive for technical as well as aesthetic reasons, the message is clear: the opulent blue pigment will appear at San Marco only on the Virgin Mary and only in the chapter room.[14]

Frescoes in the Dormitory Corridors

Of all religious orders, only the Dominicans actually legislated the use of images in their dormitories. Paintings, in other words, were essential components of the prayer, meditation, and study that went on in the seclusion of Dominican dormitories. So it is that, upstairs at San Marco, the mood and meanings of the frescoes deviate from those in the public spaces in and around the cloister (fig. 22).

In addition to their Rule, a feature they shared with all other religious orders, the Dominicans also had and still have a flexible corpus of legislation called the Constitutions. These established the complex governance system—the Order of Preachers was the only truly democratic medieval religious institution—and provided the guidelines for the daily activities of a community of men presumed to be scholars. The Dominican Constitutions are highly responsive

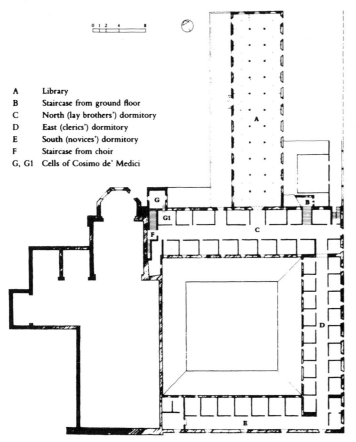

Figure 22: Florence, San Marco, reconstructed plan of 1450, first floor

to historical changes because they can be altered by the General Chapter, the main legislative body, every three years. They are, therefore, useful documents for understanding Fra Angelico's frescoes at San Marco.

Constitutions govern the use and distribution of space in a Dominican dormitory. Traditionally, monastic dormitories, such as those used by Benedictine or Cistercian monks, were simply long chambers with rows of beds down each side, used only for sleeping. But because the Dominicans were expressly charged with preaching and teaching theology, they needed places for private study, prayer, and reflection. Consequently, they invented the practice of placing rows of small cubicles or cells in the shedlike space of the dormitory itself, rather like hospital beds surrounded with curtains for privacy. Because Saint Dominic was concerned with modesty in architecture as in everything else, the Constitutions require that the walls of these cells not exceed twelve feet. By the fifteenth century, this architectural fine point had long since fallen into disuse. It comes as no surprise, however, to learn that the buildings at San Marco observe the letter as well as the spirit of the law. Thus the dormitory's interior walls are exactly twelve feet high.

The Constitutions also specify that each friar be assigned his own, private cell; the prior and the lector, who was the community's teacher, might have two cells, one for his own use and the other as an office or classroom. Each cell was to be furnished with a bed, a desk, a chair, a kneeler for prayer, and—most remarkably—an image of Christ, the Virgin Mary, or Saint Dominic for the friar to contemplate. Additionally, the dormitory corridor was to be graced with an image of the Virgin Mary.

Large Dominican communities had separate dormitories for each of the three parts of any community of friars. The youngest were the novices. These were mostly adolescent boys, at least fifteen years old but usually not much older, who were in their yearlong probationary period under the guidance, instruction, and discipline of the novice master. When they moved on and took vows of poverty, chastity, and obedience, they were known as clerics, who always made up the majority of the friars in a Dominican house. They, of course, ranged in age from teenagers to very old men, and in experience from what we might think of as university or even high school students to the equivalent of full professors. Most of the friars at San Marco, however, fell in the middle, as this was primarily a community of priests who were not known, at least as a group, for their advanced learning. Finally, men who desired to live according to the Dominican Rule and Constitutions, but who either did not wish to become priests or were considered unfit to be priests—because, for example, they were either illiterate or illegitimate—could still be full members of the Order, and were known as *conversi*, lay brothers. As San Marco, like its mother house in Fiesole, was originally planned as a small community of thirty-five to forty members, the three groups were housed together, under the same roof. However, the novices had their own corridor with cells reserved for their use, as did the clerics and lay brothers. What is more, Fra Angelico made sure that the cells in each part received

paintings tuned, as it were, to the particular requirements of their novice, cleric, or lay brother inhabitants.

At San Marco a grand staircase, rising behind the chapter room, leads to the dormitory on the second floor. From the landing visitors look up the second flight and see the beautiful *Annunciation* facing them from the wall of the north corridor (fig. 23). It is well to pause

Figure 23: Florence, San Marco, View from steps of the *Annunciation* in the north dormitory

Figure 24: Fra Angelico assistant, *Saint Dominic with the Crucifix*. Florence, San Marco, north corridor

Figure 25: Fra Angelico, *Madonna of the Shadows*. Florence, San Marco, east dormitory

here, because from the landing the doorway blocks off the painting's light source. On a sunny day one will instantly perceive how the morning light washes over that wall, and one will then see, and this perception can take one's breath away, that Fra Angelico painted his scene to look as though the natural light in the actual space of the dormitory were flooding the holy scene itself (see Pl. 10). The light melds the friars' home and the Virgin's house at Nazareth into a single dwelling.

Once in the corridor itself, opposite the *Annunciation* and just left of the entrance, one sees another version of *Saint Dominic with the Crucifix*, adapted from the huge fresco in the cloister (fig. 24). About halfway down the eastern corridor, which connects both sides of the dormitory, is another wall painting showing the Virgin and Child with a group of saints standing on either side (fig. 25). Fra Angelico painted the wall below this group to look as though it were covered with slabs of precious marbles. The light, which seems to take over the picture's surface just as it penetrated the space in the *Annunciation*, makes such a clean mark that the fresco is known, for obvious reasons, as the *Madonna of the Shadows*. Clearly, neither image of the Virgin is "just" decoration. Each, indeed, played its special role in the friars' daily life.

Frescoes in the Novices' Dormitory

At the end of the long corridor running from the *Annunciation* past the *Madonna of the Shadows* with cells on either side, another, shorter, corridor leads at right angles to a suite of three small rooms at the very end (fig. 26). It was here that the firebrand prophet Fra Girolamo Savonarola had his cell and office while prior of San Marco. In Fra Angelico's day, however, these rooms had different uses. The two small cells were storage rooms for bedding and clothing, while the larger space, which one reaches by a flight of three steps, served as the novices' meeting and classroom.

Figure 26: Florence, San Marco, south dormitory, view down corridor

38

The seven cells opening onto this corridor housed the novices. Each has a fresco showing Saint Dominic with the Crucifix. Although this subject appears elsewhere, in the novices' cells Saint Dominic's posture and actions conform to his behavior as described in a thirteenth-century manual for training novices in the ways of Dominican prayer. It is called *De Modo Orandi*, the English translation, "The Nine Ways of Prayer."[15] This text was revived by the Dominican Observance in the fifteenth century. Most interesting is the fact that the nine "ways" that Saint Dominic observed while praying are all gestural and silent. In other words, the manual does not provide verbal formulas for prayer, but postures and attitudes that may be assumed in order to achieve the desired state of mind, such as compunction, humility, or awe. This stress on the congruence between disposition and behavior is highly characteristic of Dominican psychology right from the order's beginnings, and the Observants' revival of long-neglected spiritual practices was one of many strategies whereby they sought to revivify the present by selective though faithful recourse to the past.

There is no way to know exactly how these frescoes were to be used by the novices themselves. Doubtless the novice master carefully instructed them in the nine ways of prayer, and the frescoes were there to keep the whole text, not just the particular mode exemplified in the painting, before their minds at all times. As the Constitutions required the friars to keep the doors to their cells open except while sleeping, all the novices would have seen all the frescoes as they passed back and forth through that corridor during their daily rounds.

Frescoes in the Clerics' Cells

The twenty cells on the east corridor are the most famous, not least because Fra Angelico was solely responsible for at least five of them, and he participated in the execution of several others. In general, however, the variety of subject matter and aesthetic quality encountered in the clerics' dormitory suggest a very early stage in the campaign; it seems prudent to assume that the frescoes in these twenty cells were the first to be painted anywhere at San Marco.

Fra Angelico and an assistant almost certainly began painting in Cells 10 and 11, which are connected by an arched opening (fig. 27). Located at the juncture of the clerics' and novices' dormitories, and embellished with images whose meaning is relevant to the Dominican order as well as to the consecration of youth to God, it seems likely that this, the only double cell at San Marco, was assigned to the prior. In Cell 22 at the opposite corner, the fresco's frame and subject matter—the *Virgin Mary with the Crucifix*—make it likely that the novice master was housed here, close to his charges and the prior (fig. 28). The assignment of cells elsewhere in the clerics' dormitory was almost certainly random, and we do not know even whether friars moved from cell to cell, although this seems unlikely.

Figure 27: Florence, San Marco, view of cells 10 and 11

Figure 28: Florence, San Marco, view of cell 22

Scenes of the Crucifixion in one form or another dominate the cell frescoes along the cloister side of the corridor; the simplified subjects and their workmanlike but uninspired style probably reflects Fra Angelico's decision to assign his less-skilled helpers to that area, while he himself worked with two or perhaps three assistants along the outer range. For it is here that his truly transcendent cell frescoes are found, paintings such as the *Annunciation* in Cell 3 and the *Mocking of Christ* in Cell 7 (figs. 29 and 30).

The cell frescoes in the novitiate, of course, exactly conform to the Constitutions' requirement that an image of Christ, the Virgin, or Saint Dominic appear in the cells. In the clerics' dormitory, however, that rule was amended though not broken. For apart from the variations on the Crucifixion, the subjects in the east range of cells are drawn from (but do not illustrate) scenes from the life of Christ or, in the case of the Coronation, of the Virgin. The most satisfactory explanation for these choices is to realize that these scenes also emblemize the major feasts of the liturgical year—Easter, Christmas, All Saints, and so on. Thus, although the frescoes may not precisely conform to the Constitutions' dictates, they satisfy the spirit of those requirements and even go beyond them. As an Order of Preachers, and as contemplatives, the Dominicans were accus-

tomed to meditating on Christ's life through the language and images of the liturgy itself. Thus, using the calendar as a guide in the selection of themes for the cell frescoes provided enough uniformity and enough variety. We do not know how the selection process went or who took part in it. But remembering that the San Marco com-

Figure 29: Fra Angelico, *Annunciation*. Florence, San Marco, cell 3

Figure 30: Fra Angelico, *Mocking of Christ*. Florence, San Marco, cell 7

munity was very, very small and that Fra Angelico knew each friar intimately, we may safely imagine that he chose the subjects in consultation with the friars themselves.

What connects the clerics' frescoes with the novices' is the text of *De Modo Orandi*. For each cleric saw not only an image referring to a feast of Christ on his wall, he saw that image mediated by the presence of a Dominican model, usually Saint Dominic or Saint Peter Martyr. And that model always, in every case, is shown in one of the nine modes of prayer learned in the novices' year of training. Thus, the biblical passages as well as the feasts that commemorate the events of Christ's life were subjected, through the images themselves, to Observant Dominican habits of prayer and meditation.

Frescoes in the Cells on the North Corridor

Lay brothers did not participate as active ministers and preachers in the liturgy as did the literate clerics. They participated silently because they were assumed to be illiterate and thus unable to follow the complex rituals accompanying the clerics and novices' common prayer. This distinction between the learned and the unlearned is echoed in the frescoes in those cells on the north corridor assigned to lay brothers, along the wall where Fra Angelico painted the *Annunciation* (fig. 31). These are far more narrative in manner, as their burden was to remind the beholder of stories rather than of theological or mystical verities.

Figure 31: Florence, San Marco, view down the north corridor

Figure 32: Fra Angelico assistant, *Crucifixion*. Florence, San Marco, cell 37

Figure 33(right): Fra Angelico assistant, *Communion of the Apostles*.
Florence, San Marco, cell 35

The architectural plan parallels the novices' dormitory on the south. At the end of the north corridor, next to the doorway leading to the friars' staircase into the church, is an odd-shaped cell, number 37. Its fresco, a *Crucifixion*, recalls the same scene in the chapter room and suggests that this was the lay brothers' meeting room (fig. 32). Likewise, the fresco in Cell 1 is a scene from the Passion of Christ, which begins with the Last Supper (at San Marco, it is the *Communion of the Apostles* in Cell 35) and ends with Christ's appearance to Saint Mary Magdalene in the Garden of Gethsemane (figs. 33 and 34). This scene, called the *Noli Me Tangere*, is the

Figure 34: Fra Angelico assistant, *Noli Me Tangere*. Florence, San Marco, cell 1

subject of Cell 1, one of the clerics' cells. However, in style and composition the painting belongs with the cells on the north corridor, and for that reason one may assume that the lay brothers' master was housed there, just as the novice master occupied the corresponding cell at the diagonally opposite end of the clerics' dormitory.

Figure 35: Fra Angelico assistant, *Sermon on the Mount*. Florence, San Marco, cell 31

Figure 36: Florence, San Marco, view into cells 38 and 39

Other cells on the north corridor had other functions. The fresco in Cell 31 shows the *Sermon on the Mount*; its large size and its location close to the library suggest that it was the lector's classroom (fig. 35). And the cells along the north wall—Cells 40 through 45—may have functioned as storerooms, guest rooms, or offices. Certainly Cells 38 and 39 are highly peculiar (fig. 36), They are conjoined, and an inscription clearly states that they were the quarters reserved for Cosimo de' Medici's use when he visited San Marco. The frescoes in these two cells, furthermore, make the Medicean connection, even specifically to Cosimo himself, unmistakable and repeat, here in the most private part of the complex, something of the political realities that underlay the Dominicans' life of prayer and meditation.

IV. Fra Angelico's Technique

*F*rescoes are to painting what soufflés are to cooking. The ingredients are few; putting them together is simple; and the results can be spectacular if everything goes right. But there's the rub. One blunder and disaster is certain, because both frescoes and soufflés are hypersensitive to mishandling. Both require careful planning, deft handling, and the ability to think fast. In other words, cooks and painters have to know exactly what they are doing at each stage of the procedure. Fra Angelico did, and just as a great soufflé chef can coax new flavors and textures out of eggs, Fra Angelico uncovered expressive potentials in the fresco medium that no master before him, not even Masaccio, had found.

In its own way, this fact is as astounding about Fra Angelico as it is about Michelangelo's work on the Sistine Chapel ceiling, because neither artist had a great deal of documented experience in fresco technique before embarking on his respective masterpiece. In Michelangelo's case, of course, we know that he was Ghirlandaio's pupil while that master was working on frescoes at Santa Maria Novella. But no such relationship corresponds for Fra Angelico, who was trained as a manuscript illuminator and painter of tempera panels. It might be observed that the Camaldolese monk Lorenzo Monaco painted in all three media, and it is likely that Fra Angelico was at least introduced to fresco painting while in training. However, nothing prepares one for his astonishing mastery of that technique, his almost bravura way with paint, which one finds at San Marco.

Frescoes are not only aesthetically architectural, they are *literally* architectural. The painter begins with a wall prepared with a coat of coarse plaster, often containing bristle to increase its tooth, called *arriccio*. On this layer most artists placed their rough designs, first in charcoal and then retraced with a brush dipped in red-earth pigment. These preliminary sketches, which also include the guidelines for any architectural settings the painting will have, are called *sinopie* after the color of the pigment. Once in place, the *sinopia* would be gradually covered by the finished painting.

The Italian word *fresco* means "wet" or "cool," indicating not the paint but the surface to which the paint is applied. In this case, the surface is a finely ground plaster often mixed with marble dust to increase its smoothness. The artist applied this plaster, called *intonaco*, in very thin layers to the *arriccio*, whose rough surface provided the necessary adhesion. After paper became widely available in large sheets at an affordable cost, artists tended to abandon the *sinopia* method of transferring the design. They turned instead to the more exact device of the cartoon, which is a full-scale drawing on paper. The cartoon was laid over the *intonaco* and the design transferred by incising a sharp line all around the drawing. Alternatively, the outlines of the drawing could be punched with a needle and then a bag of charcoal dust tapped lightly over these punch marks to transfer the design as a series of dots, called *spolveri*, onto the *intonaco*.

At San Marco there is no trace of Fra Angelico's having used cartoons. It is almost certain that he made *sinopia* drawings on the *arriccio*. The *intonaco* layer can be removed from the *arriccio*, as conservators were constrained to do on some other artists' frescoes, for example, after Florence was flooded in 1966; but because the frescoes at San Marco have never been disturbed, their layers of *arriccio*—and, along with them, whatever underdrawings there may have been—have never been exposed.

The paint used in these mural paintings, like all paint, is made of a colored powder or pigment suspended in a medium that makes it into a liquid which, when dry, becomes a paint film. In the case of tempera, this binding medium is egg yolk; in oil painting, it is nut or seed oil; in manuscript illumination, it is gum arabic. In fresco painting, the binding medium is glue and limewater. Once applied to wet plaster, therefore, the limewater causes the paint to bind with the wall itself. When dry, a traditionally applied fresco painting (known as *buon fresco*) becomes an actual part of the wall and cannot be separated from the *intonaco*. This means, of course, that the artist can work on an area only as large as he can finish in one session, as both the paint and plaster are quick to dry. It also means that painters cannot make mistakes, change their minds, or paint only when "inspired." Fresco technique is ruthlessly unforgiving of technical errors.

Painters planned their work, therefore, to be executed in patches of fresh plaster, called *giornate* after the Italian word meaning a "day's length." Furthermore, because a new, wet, *giornata* always abutted a dry one, it left a visible border, allowing one to trace the progress of work from top to bottom by counting these patches. The number of *giornate* in any given painting will also tell one how many working sessions went into the execution, remembering that it was possible to paint more than one giornata in a summer's long working day. Finally, the *giornate* also tell one just how deliberately the artist proceeded. Most of the cell frescoes at San Marco, for instance, were carried out in three or four *giornate*. But the great *Transfiguration* in Cell 6 required no fewer then eight, one for Christ's head alone. This technical aspect, then, reveals something of the artist's interests and intentions.

Certain pigments must be applied to dry plaster because they react destructively with wet lime. Using these colors required painters to go over surfaces finished in *buon fresco* to touch up or enhance original passages, or to add ones that would be in a particular hue. In cases where the paint is applied to a dry wall, the technique is known as *fresco a secco*, and the paint layers are just as subject to peeling and flaking as are those in tempera or oil.

The huge majority of paintings at San Marco were carried out in the traditional *buon fresco* method, but there are some interesting exceptions. Most remarkable of these is the *Madonna of the Shadows*. In the course of conservation measures carried out in the early 1980s, it was discovered that the panels imitating colored marbles in the lower half were made, as one would expect, in *buon fresco*. The composition itself, however, has a faint underpainting in *buon fresco* that Fra Angelico then overlayed with tempera, the medium used for panel paintings. Almost certainly, he did this for aesthetic reasons. We have already noticed that the only ultramarine blue at San Marco is in the chapter room's *Crucifixion*. Upstairs, the pigments are uniformly inexpensive earth tones, even in pictures showing the Madonna, except for the *Madonna of the Shadows* (see Pl. 15). The vibrant reds in that painting, on Saint Lawrence's dalmatic, for example, are made with a pigment that must be suspended in egg yolk or oil. Furthermore, the surfaces of tempera paintings have a sheen and brilliance unmatched by fresco. Here, in other words, Fra Angelico wanted the visual sumptuousness of tempera because the painting, as we shall see, was intended to recall the altarpiece he had made for the church.

Other displays of technical virtuosity abound. In the *Transfiguration* of Cell 6 and the *Coronation of the Virgin* in Cell 9, Fra Angelico used the actual cream-colored *intonaco* as the white background (see Pls. 27 and 29). This allowed him to apply the genuine, brighter, white pigment to symbolize the divine light shining through Christ's face and garments in the *Transfiguration*, or the sacred radiance falling on Christ and the Virgin in the *Coronation*. In the *Annunciation* for Cell 3, he left completely uncovered the red-earth underdrawing for the Virgin's blue mantle (see Pl. 32). Of course, the color harmonizes wonderfully with the palette in the rest of the painting—one imagines that blue would be too strong here—but the deliberate eschewing of the traditional color becomes a painterly symbol of the Virgin's humility, which is the central message of this particular cell fresco. In the *Annunciation* at the top of the stairs in the north corridor, Fra Angelico went in the opposite direction. While maintaining his rule of avoiding expensive pigments, he nonetheless managed to embellish the angel's wings by stirring silica into the paint (see Pl. 13). When one stands in front of the painting, something invisible in photographs happens: the wings wink and sparkle.

Finally, it is clear, when one is actually present in the cells, that Fra Angelico loved the act of painting. The background of the Cell 3 *Annunciation* is a cascade of gossamer pastels. Christ's face in the

Cell 6 *Transfiguration* was so painstakingly made that Fra Angelico devoted an entire working day to it alone (see Pl. 28). And the poignancy of the sweet tones of Christ's head against the acrid green of the cloth behind him in the Cell 7 *Mocking of Christ* is an exact visual analogue of the bitter humiliation that the scene symbolizes (see Pl. 31).

People are often disappointed when they learn that Renaissance artists were matter-of-fact businessmen who practiced their trade in a competitive money economy and who belonged to guilds that were the equivalent of today's trade associations, that is, designed to keep prices up and control competition. They worked under contract rather than on speculation, and their products were designed to address their patrons' concerns, not their own. These facts fly in the face of our notions of what art is about, or somehow should be about, because most of us nourish a romantic (and modern) fantasy in which artists are lonely visionaries whose work reveals their deepest and most private selves. This is simply not true of fifteenth-century painters.

No matter how supernal the beauty of Fra Angelico's art, in fact, nothing allows us to say that he was any different from his colleagues in most of these ways. He ran a large and highly efficient shop that produced work of superb technical quality at a regular clip. What is more, even this cursory glance at his creative mind shows that he strove to be in the vanguard of contemporary developments in Florentine painting. He was as levelheaded as any jewelry merchant on the Ponte Vecchio and no stranger to professional ambition.

All of that said, it must also be allowed that Fra Angelico has always spoken to ordinary men and women at a depth that few other artists of any period have plumbed. Even by 1500, when taste had changed radically and painters of Fra Angelico's generation were looked on as old-fashioned and out of date, the resale of his work brought high prices. Closer to our own time, George Eliot wrote her novel *Romola* with a copy of a fresco by Fra Angelico before her eyes, so that it would keep her mindful of the Renaissance sensibility she was trying to evoke in her story. People have always discovered that his paintings summon a vague longing from somewhere deep in their hearts. It isn't easy to say just what that longing is, even when it is one's own heart that is doing the longing. But no one can spend an hour watching the summertime crowds troop through the San Marco Museum without observing Fra Angelico's singular power to move even the most jaded and bored of tourists to something that looks, from the outside anyway, close to the threshold of bliss.

To be sure, this is partly accountable to the wonderful state of San Marco's preservation, itself a testimony to the Florentines' long love affair with Fra Angelico, whom they called "Blessed" (*Beato*)

Angelico for centuries before Pope John Paul II officially beatified him in 1983. It is partly because the frescoes look today much the way they did when Fra Angelico finished them. This is due not only to the expert and even loving restoration and cleaning they underwent in the 1970s and 1980s by the late Dino Dini. It is also a testimony to the enduring qualities of fresco technique, and particularly when applied by the gentle but knowing hand of a great artist. But in the end, there is no explaining Fra Angelico's power. Who would want to anyhow? It's better just to go to San Marco and see for yourself.

Notes to the Introduction

1. Apart from Benozzo Gozzoli, Fra Angelico's best-known follower, who was responsible for many frescoes in the north dormitory, the identity and number of his assistants remain unknown. As no records document Fra Angelico's activity at San Marco, one must work with secondary evidence. That provides the plausible, but by no means proven, supposition that the decoration of San Marco proceeded piecemeal, in stages when the warm weather allowed fresco painting. For about two years after 1438, when Cosimo de' Medici acquired the rights to put up his own altarpiece in the chancel of San Marco, Fra Angelico was busy with that project. Thus, he probably turned to the mural paintings only in the spring of 1440 or 1441. He hired a large group of experienced painters to work with him, and—technically speaking—they could easily have carried out the work in the cloister, chapter room, refectory, and clerics' dormitory in two seasons, although we know that the chapter room was not painted until after the winter of 1443. The frescoes in the north dormitory, where the library is found, and in the novices' cells in the south dormitory probably date much later, to a time after 1450.

2. For a full discussion of these matters, see Hood 1993, pp. 29–38.

3. The standard edition compares the two versions: Vasari, Giorgio, *Le vite de' più eccellenti architetti, pittori, e scultori italiani* (1550 and 1568), ed. R. Bettarini and P. Barocchi (Florence: Sansoni, 1971). A handy, though abridged, translation is Vasari, Giorgio, *Lives of the Artists*, trans. G. Bull (New York: Penguin Books, 1965).

4. For a fuller account, with references, see Hood 1993, pp. 7–13.

5. Recently, Carl Brandon Strehlke has reopened the discussion of Fra Angelico's beginnings with a series of highly interesting arguments and reattributions of works rarely, if ever, associated with the artist's name. To my eye, there is not enough correspondence between Lorenzo Monaco and Fra Angelico to support Strehlke's thesis that the former was the latter's teacher. It seems to me that Fra Angelico's master, if he may be specified at all, was likely in his immediate ambient, perhaps Biaggio Sanguigni, whose son, also a miniaturist slightly older than Fra Angelico, was the artist's friend. See Strehlke 1994.

6. Although now cut out of the original manuscript, we know that the initial originally appeared on folio 3 and that its letter, *A*, began the first responsory for the first nocturn of Easter: "Angelus Domini descendit de celo et accedens revolvit lapidem et super eum sedit" [An Angel of the Lord came down from heaven and drawing near rolled back the stone and sat upon it]. Paris, Musée du Louvre, Cabinet des Dessins (R.F. 830). For the text and a detailed discussion of this miniature, see *Painting and Illumination*, cat. no. 29a, pp. 237–38.

7. *Painting and Illumination*, cat. no. 48, fol. 33v, pp. 332–39.

8. *Painting and Illumination*, cat. no. 48, fol. 41v, pp. 333–34.

9. For a full discussion of this and the altarpiece for San Pier Martire, see Hood 1993, pp. 65–77.

10. See Gilbert 1984.

11. For the most recent scholarship on Zanobi Strozzi, see Carl Brandon Strehlke's catalogue entries in *Painting and Illumination*, pp. 349–61.

12. I am grateful to my friend Thomas Van Nortwick for his help in what is not such a simple translation. "*Tuis*" in the second line, for example, has no specific antecedent.

13. There are, it is true, museums where frescoes are displayed out of their original contexts. In every case I know of, however, removing the frescoes was an urgent matter of protecting them from total ruin. Although there are exceptions to the rule that frescoes must be studied *in situ*, those are mercifully few.

14. Fra Angelico also painted a Crucifixion (or Crucifix, the documents are not clear) on the end wall of the refectory. However, the wall was torn down when the room was enlarged in 1524, and along with it went the fresco. It is almost certain that the present fresco, by Sogliani, preserves something of Fra Angelico's composition, but it is impossible to be more specific than that.

15. For Simon Tugwell's excellent translation of *De Modo Orandi*, see "The Nine Ways of Prayer."

PLATES AND COMMENTARIES

PLATE 1

Saint Dominic with the Crucifix

AT THE TIME WHEN FRA ANGELICO WORKED AT SAN MARCO, THERE was a kind of "boom" in Florentine cloister decoration. Painters of contemporary projects at the Badia Fiorentina, San Miniato al Monte, and elsewhere generally covered the cloister walls with frescoes. Not Fra Angelico. Apart from the five overdoor lunettes, this is the only original fresco in the cloister at San Marco, now surrounded by a seventeenth-century frame and figures of the Virgin Mary and Saint John painted on either side at the time the frame was installed. The starkness of Fra Angelico's composition is all the more apparent because of its great size—the figures are scaled to life. In spite of Fra Angelico's fidelity to the actual appearance of real human bodies, this painting is not a "scene." It represents instead a psychological or spiritual ideal, which is the relationship between the friars at San Marco and the Crucified Savior. The emphasis on asceticism—voluntary hardships undertaken for the sake of spiritual growth—was a hallmark of the Dominican Observance. As the order's founder, Saint Dominic is here shown as the embodiment of its ideals.

PLATE 2

Saint Dominic with the Crucifix (detail of Saint Dominic)

DESPITE ITS SIZE, THE DETAILS OF THIS FRESCO ARE AS CAREFULLY rendered as though it were a small panel painting intended for viewing at close range. In this way it is highly distinct from, say, Masaccio's frescoes in the Brancacci Chapel, where the artist represented the planes of heads in broad, almost sculptural, strokes of light and dark paint. In this head of Saint Dominic, by contrast, Fra Angelico showed the founder's face with minute detail, weeping and swept away by a surge of strong emotion. Because the fresco is right next to the friars' entrance to the church and the figure of Saint Dominic is just above eye level, it seems clear that Fra Angelico intended his painting to remind the friars of Saint Dominic's own prayer life. Descriptions of the saint alone in prayer survived, and most of them report that he prayed before a crucifix with sighing and weeping, as here. The artist even based the physiognomy on Saint Dominic's appearance as carefully described by a thirteenth-century writer.

PLATE 3

Saint Dominic with the Crucifix (detail of Christ)

Just as for the figure of Saint Dominic, Fra Angelico based his representation of Christ on studies from a live model, in this case nude. Although an unusual process for artists at this date, nothing else can explain the exactness with which the painter described the layers of bone, muscle, and skin in the upper torso. Indeed, Fra Angelico was so determined to show Jesus as fully human that he even gave Christ body hair, another extraordinary move in consideration of the time and place. All of these, of course, are strategies for raising the invisible realities of Saint Dominic's—and, by extension, each friar's—mystical identity with Christ to the fully realized plane of actual experience. To this end, he even showed Christ as not yet dead. His eyes are slightly open and his lips parted, as though he were looking at and speaking to Saint Dominic, kneeling at the foot of the Cross.

PLATE 4
Crucifixion (in the chapter room)

ONLY THE CHURCH ITSELF WAS MORE SACRED TO A MONASTIC community than the chapter room. Not only did all important institutional assemblies gather there, but the community met every morning in the chapter room to conduct its business. Some of this was purely practical. Other business, particularly the daily Chapter of Faults, governed the moral life of the whole community. During this part of the morning's proceedings, individual friars confessed to infractions of the Rule and Constitutions, however minor. The major purpose of the Chapter of Faults was to assure the community's harmony and peace. According to Dominican teaching, in fact, a friar's private relationship with God was directly affected by his willingness and ability to live charitably with others.

The chapter room was also open to anyone from the outside who had gained admission to the cloister. The decoration, therefore, invariably communicated something about the order to which the particular chapter room belonged and, usually, about the resident community. In every case, however, the main image in a chapter room was a Crucifixion, and at San Marco, Fra Angelico brought all these themes together in a single monumental image that fills the entire wall opposite the entrance. It not only relates the central message of Christ's death, but it also connects that event to the Dominican Observance and even to the convent of San Marco as it was constituted about 1450.

PLATE 5

Crucifixion (detail of pelican in the border)

HEADS OF PROPHETS AND A SIBYL PROJECT THROUGH TEN OF THE eleven diamond-shaped openings in the border around the fresco of the *Crucifixion.* They hold scrolls with Latin inscriptions, drawn mostly from the Hebrew Scriptures, which could be used for meditating on Christ's Passion. In the center at the top, however, appears a pelican (clearly, Fra Angelico had never seen a real one) with her chicks. An old wives' tale says that pelicans feed their young with blood torn from their own breasts, and thus images like this became emblems of the relationship between Christ's willing sacrifice on the Cross and his feeding the faithful on his own Body and Blood in the Eucharist. Here, Fra Angelico glossed this favorite device with the inscription running just below. Taken from Psalm 101, it translates: "I have become like a pelican in the wilderness," thereby underscoring the emotional cost, in human terms, of the theological realities that the image symbolizes.

Further, the image of the pelican is at the summit of a vertical axis running down through Christ's Cross and terminating with the

head of Saint Dominic in the center of the Dominican Vine at the bottom. When the friars assembled in the chapter room, the prior sat immediately below. Thus, the alignment of images of self-giving passed from the abstraction of the pelican motif, through Christ and Saint Dominic, right into the actual human being, the prior, who represented both the founder and the Savior to the gathered brethren.

Plate 6
Crucifixion (detail of Biblical Saints)

FIFTEENTH-CENTURY ARTISTS WERE CAREFUL TO MAKE CLEAR distinctions between "real" and "ideal" people in their paintings. Although the two thieves are biblical characters, even Saint Dysmas was never the focus of a widespread or active cult, and therefore Fra Angelico felt free to depict them in all their fragile humanity. Not so the group of mourners gathered at the left of Christ's Cross. In the center of this group the Virgin Mary is shown collapsing with grief, supported by Saint John, Saint Mary Clopas, and the kneeling Saint Mary Magdalene. These four are of course biblical witnesses of Christ's death, and each was highly venerated from the earliest times. Consequently, Fra Angelico drew their faces from his repertory of standardized though ideally beautiful physiognomies that he used on altarpieces. Further, the saints' garments are rendered in clear and precious colors. Fra Angelico used ultramarine blue for the only time at San Marco on the Virgin's cloak, vermilion red and malachite green on the other women. Even so, the facial expressions and gestures are eloquent of sorrow. Indeed, the kneeling monastic saints on the right side of the composition look, when at all, at the Virgin and not at the Cross. Their own grief, in other words, is shown to be a sympathetic response to hers.

PLATE 7

Crucifixion (detail of the Good and Bad Thieves)

JUST AS FOR THE FIGURES OF CHRIST AND SAINT DOMINIC IN THE cloister, Fra Angelico chose the life-size scale for those in the *Crucifixion*, thereby strengthening the psychological link between viewers and painting mentioned in the commentary on a previous detail (see Pl. 5). Furthermore, some—though not all—of these figures are obviously based on life studies. He seems to have recruited grown men, rather than the adolescent shop assistants who usually doubled as artists' models in the period, to pose for the thieves hanging on either side of Christ. The lift of the rib cage and the tautness of muscle and sinews cannot have been the painter's invention. But nowhere more than in these two figures did Fra Angelico use facial expressions to greater effect. The repentant thief on Christ's right, whom legend named Saint Dysmas, reflects the fifteenth-century ideal of refined masculine beauty, including the long nose, high cheekbones, and blond hair. Fra Angelico followed the period's stereotypical class distinctions in the physiognomy of the other thief, who is depicted as swarthy and coarse-featured. But his agonized expression is a masterpiece of visual communication, and it demonstrates Fra Angelico's abilities in describing profound psychological states, an accomplishment that made him unique among Florentine painters of his generation.

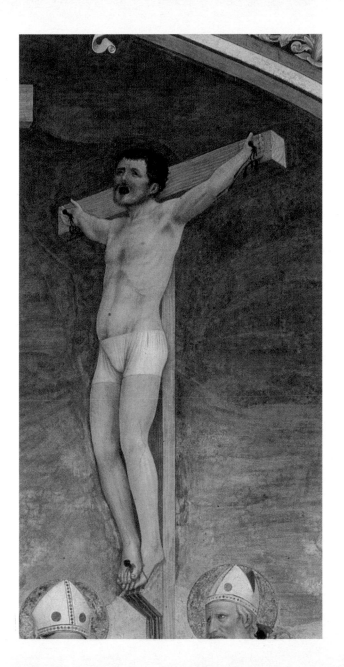

PLATE 8

Crucifixion (detail of Monastic Saints)

ON THE RIGHT, FRA ANGELICO PLACED SAINT DOMINIC, THE FOUNDER of the Order of Preachers, and Saint Augustine, nominal author of its Rule, closest to Christ's Cross, as was appropriate for the two most prominent saints in a Dominican convent. Beyond them, nine others stand or kneel. From left to right, these are Saint Jerome, translator of the Bible into Latin and legendary founder of an order of hermits; Saint Anthony Abbot, a great desert ascetic; Saint Francis of Assisi; Saint Benedict, father of Western monasticism; Saint Bernard of Clairvaux, the great twelfth-century Cistercian much admired by the Dominicans; Saint John Gualbert, kneeling, the founder of a monastery of reform Benedictines at Vallombrosa, near Florence; Saint Romuald, founder of Camaldoli, another monastery near Florence; and, finally, the two other major Dominican saints in the period, Peter Martyr, who was assassinated by an ax blow to the head, and Thomas Aquinas. Aquinas's famous corpulence obviously inspired Fra Angelico's representation, and it seems plain that the artist sought out others—perhaps friars at San Marco—who would suit his mental image of one or another saint. For here, too, the expressions of sorrow are too nicely observed, and the characterizations too finely drawn, for there not to have been living models who sat for what amounts to portraits. The impact of seeing familiar faces transposed into a representation of such solemnity and size must have been extremely powerful for Fra Angelico's fellow Dominicans.

PLATE 9

Crucifixion (detail of Saints Cosmas, Damian, Lawrence, Mark, and John the Baptist)

IT COMES AS SOMETHING OF A SURPRISE TO REALIZE THAT ONLY Dominic, of the eleven monastic saints, actually looks at Christ. Those that look across the composition fix their gaze on the Virgin Mary, but most are shown as though Christ's death were present in their minds rather than their eyes. Glances and their direction are extremely important for understanding Fra Angelico's *Crucifixion*, and therefore the great contrast between the left and right sides of the composition must be understood as not only deliberate but significant. The monastic reformers were not only models for the Dominican Observance as an institution. Their individual sanctity, particularly as focused here on the Passion, was an ideal for each friar. The saints on the left side of the *Crucifixion*, however, had no particular importance for Dominicans. Their presence is, instead, a sign of the intimate relationship between ecclesiastical and political institutions in pre-Enlightenment Europe. Cosmas and Damian, known as healing saints, are shown wearing the gray tunics and red, fur-lined mantles that identified physicians in fifteenth-century Florence. They were Medici patron saints; as Cosimo de' Medici was in turn San Marco's patron, they appear in the chapter room as well as on the high altarpiece that Fra Angelico made for the church. Likewise, Saint Lawrence, shown with the grill on which he was martyred, wears a deacon's dalmatic; he was the titular patron of San Lorenzo, the Medici family's parish church a few blocks away. Saint John the Baptist, standing at the right edge, was the patron of Florence itself. He and Saint Mark, kneeling, look out of the picture and gesture, Saint John to the Cross and Saint Mark to his gospel, which once bore a text that was almost certainly derived from Mark's account of the Crucifixion.

Plate 10

Annunciation (in the north corridor)

THIS IS ONE OF FRA ANGELICO'S BEST-LOVED FRESCOES, AND FOR good reason. The theme of the Annunciation was a favorite among Observant Dominicans, who liked to imagine their priories as places where the Lord would choose to dwell. And they also strove to imitate the Virgin Mary's humility and innocence when she consented to become Christ's mother. Fra Angelico painted the subject numerous times on altarpieces and manuscripts, and there are two frescoes of the *Annunciation* in the dormitory at San Marco. He liked to place the Virgin and Angel in a walled garden, which was itself a symbol of Mary. In this painting, even the column capitals are derived from the cloister of San Marco, and the little room opening off the back looks like a friar's cell.

This image greeted the friars when they ascended the staircase from the cloister. The artist took pains to give the painting its uncanny sense of presence, which one can perceive even in a photograph. The frame was painted to look like the actual *pietra serena* moldings that articulate the wall. The internal measurements were derived from the proportions of the actual architecture and the perspective's high vanishing-point calibrated to make viewers look into a space that seems to include them. Finally and most remarkably, the light falls across the painting from the east—tradition said that the Annunciation happened at dawn—and the painted architecture is shaded so as to make it appear that the actual light in the dormitory is also the light *inside* the picture.

PLATE 11

Annunciation (detail of inscriptions)

THERE ARE TWO INSCRIPTIONS ON THE *Annunciation*. THE TOP one quotes a hymn to the Virgin and was painted at the same time as the inscription on the *Saint Dominic with the Crucifix* diagonally opposite, probably in the 1490s. The lower one, in black letters, was applied by Fra Angelico himself. In Latin, it reads: VIRGINIS INTACTE CVM VENERIS ANTE FIGVRAM PRETEREVNDO CAVE NE SILEATVR AVE, which translates: "When you come before the image of the Ever-Virgin, take care that you do not neglect to say an 'Ave.'" This, of course, is a reminder, and it tells the modern beholder that the friars prayed before this picture every time they came into the dormitory. The words are known as the Angelic Salutation: "Hail Mary, full of grace, the Lord is with you." As we also know that friars genuflected when they said this prayer, Fra Angelico's painting encouraged each Dominican to repeat not only Gabriel's words but his gesture. Almost every fresco in the dormitory, in fact, was intended to provoke some kind of action, as well as (silent) speech. For that reason, we need to understand the paintings not as mere decoration, but as integral parts of the friars' routine spiritual commerce.

PLATE 12
Annunciation (detail of Virgin Mary)

DOMINICAN COMMUNITIES WERE HEADED BY PRIORS, WHOM THE clerics elected for limited terms and whose authority was strictly circumscribed. This set the friars apart from monks, who were ruled by an abbot appointed for life and into whose hands absolute and unquestioned authority was placed. An old Dominican custom turned the monks' monarchical form of governance into a kind of spiritual metaphor, because it maintained that the Virgin Mary herself was the "Abbess" of every priory. Although she sits on a simple three-legged stool and not a throne, Fra Angelico showed the Virgin's status as Abbess through the ancient device of relative size. It is only when one measures the dimensions of the Virgin in this fresco against the scales of Angel Gabriel and, above all, against the architecture that her enormous, even disproportionate, stature becomes apparent. To underscore her office, Fra Angelico departed from the traditional color scheme for her clothing. He gave her instead a white dress and a dark, almost black, mantle. By these alterations he made the Virgin's garments appear as variations on the black-and-white Dominican habit.

PLATE 13
Annunciation (detail of Angel Gabriel)

RENAISSANCE PAINTERS IN GENERAL, AND FRA ANGELICO IN particular, were by modern standards hypersensitive to the pictorial significance of appropriate painting materials. In the simplest terms, this usually meant that the higher the rank of a personage, the more sumptuously he or she would be represented in a work of art. At San Marco, Fra Angelico carried this traditional principle even further, by maintaining a strict hierarchy of pictorial richness in conformity with their location. Thus, the high altarpiece for San Marco, today a tragic ruin, was originally the most dazzling of all Fra Angelico's paintings, full of brilliant color, gold leaf, intricate detail, and luxuriously painted fabrics. The paintings in the cloister are far less sumptuous, although a spot of ultramarine does appear in the chapter room *Crucifixion*. Just so, the simplicity and economy of the cell frescoes is extreme, out of respect for the friars' own simplicity and poverty. The corridor paintings of the *Annunciation* and the *Madonna of the Shadows*, however, received special if economical embellishments. Fra Angelico applied mordant gilt, a kind of liquid gold, to the angel's halo and garment; he gave the wings a variety of colors and even mixed silica into the *intonaco* so that the wings would glitter, an effect impossible to capture with a camera.

PLATE 14

Saint Dominic with the Crucifix
(in the north corridor)

TWO OF THE THREE FRESCOES IN THE DORMITORY CORRIDOR WERE designed to recall paintings in the public parts of the convent. This one, of course, is a version of the large composition in the cloister, rendered by a skilled assistant of Fra Angelico, perhaps Benozzo Gozzoli. Gone, however, is the sky-blue field that fills the upper part of the composition in the cloister. In the dormitory, the artists observed the utmost frugality in the use of pigments, especially blue, which was relatively costly even when not the precious ultramarine. The white background is the unpainted *intonaco* itself, its deployment as "color" one of Fra Angelico's innovations at San Marco. The red-and-green rectangular frame links this painting to the frescoes in the novices' cells, all of which show *Saint Dominic with the Crucifix* painted on bare *intonaco*. The inscription on the bottom edge was added later; the style of writing dates it to the late fifteenth century, almost certainly to the 1490s when Savonarola was prior. It quotes the opening lines of a famous hymn often sung on the Feast of the True Cross in September and suggests that the friars at San Marco in Savonarola's day held the dormitory frescoes in great respect.

PLATE 15

Madonna of the Shadows
(view from the east corridor)

THE *Annunciation* SERVED THE FRIARS BY PRESENTING THE VIRGIN Mary and the angel Gabriel as particular models for their outward behavior and their inner tranquility. The painting known as the *Madonna of the Shadows* in the east corridor performed an altogether different function. Situated in the middle of the clerics' dormitory and illuminated by hanging lamps whose brackets can still be seen in the roof beams overhead, this painting was the gathering place for the clerics and novices (but not the lay brothers), who said a group of early-morning prayers known as the Little Office in the dormitory rather than in the church. The sumptuous panels of fictive marble that form the dado were discovered only when the painting was cleaned in the early 1980s.

PLATE 16

Madonna of the Shadows

A COMPARISON WITH THE SAN MARCO ALTARPIECE SHOWS THAT the *Madonna of the Shadows* is a reduced and simplified version of that painting. As focal points for the friars' common worship, whether in the church or dormitory, this is fitting. The eight saints shown flanking the Madonna and Child, furthermore, recall the *Crucifixion* in the chapter room, as all but one appear there as well. Just as Saints Cosmas and Damian figure on the altarpiece and in the chapter room, so, too, Cosimo's own patrons appear in the *Madonna of the Shadows*, along with Saint Peter Martyr, who does double duty as a Dominican and as patron saint of Cosimo's son, Piero. The saint who does *not* appear in the chapter room is the gospel-writer standing just right of the throne, an exact pendant for the figure of Saint Mark on the left, whose open book exposes the text of his gospel. This must be Saint John the Evangelist, the patron of Cosimo's father, Giovanni de' Medici. Thus three generations of Medici men, along with the whole family through the presence of Saint Lawrence, would be remembered in the friars' prayers every morning when they grouped around the painting for the Little Office. It is worth noticing that the saints in the altarpiece are settled out-of-doors in a verdant landscape. In the *Madonna of the Shadows* they stand before a white wall ornamented with elegant classicizing details whose sharp projections give the painting its nickname.

PLATE 17

Madonna of the Shadows (detail of Christ Child)

THIS DETAIL SHOWS THAT THE *Madonna of the Shadows* IS THE most technically complex painting at San Marco because it is a hybrid. Like all the other compositions in the dormitory, the foundation was painted in *buon fresco*. Then, however, Fra Angelico re-covered the entire surface with egg tempera, as though it were a panel painting. In the Christ Child's garments can still be seen the pale ochre outlines with which Fra Angelico sketched the figures and architecture directly onto the fresh *intonaco*. In the shadows of the Christ Child's face the earth-green pigment that covered all the flesh areas shows through the pink tones. His tunic was originally blue, but because it and the rose-madder tones of the Christ Child's mantle were painted *a secco*, most of the original color has flaked off. This highly unusual choice was almost certainly a consequence of the artist's feeling it necessary to give this composition some of the coloristic richness of its model, the altarpiece. Tempera not only allowed him to use some brilliant pigments, like cinnabar red, which are unstable in fresco, it also permitted him to build up layers of transparent areas, one on top of the other, which he could not have done to such effect in *buon fresco*. The exquisite, opalescent hues of the Christ Child's face are direct consequences of this innovation in the venerable technical traditions of mural painting.

PLATE 18

Madonna of the Shadows (detail of Saint Dominic)

NOWHERE ELSE IN ALL HIS WORK DID FRA ANGELICO SHOW SAINT Dominic holding and pointing to an open book, on which is written a stern, even terrifying, warning. It says: CARITATEM HABETE HVMILITATEM SERVATE PAVPERTATEM VOLVNTARIAM POS- SIDETE. MALEDICTIONEM DEI ET MEAM IMPRECOR POSSES- SIONES INDVCENTIBVS IN HOC ORDINE. ["Have charity; preserve humility; possess voluntary poverty. I invoke God's curse and mine on the introduction of possessions into this order."] These words were known as "Saint Dominic's Curse," and although they did not appear in the order's official biography of its founder, a thirteenth- century life of Saint Dominic claimed that Saint Dominic said these things on his deathbed.

It seems that this inscription was Fra Angelico's idea and that its sentiments reflected his own. By 1450, the time when this painting was made, the community of San Marco did, in fact, own income- producing possessions. That meant that it had broken from one of the Observance's strongest (though not legally binding) principles, namely, institutional poverty. Fra Angelico's own community of San Domenico in Fiesole, however, did not own income-producing property and even refused such benefices at just the time that the artist made this painting. In conjunction with the Medici patron saints, whom Fra Angelico was required to include, the figure of Saint Dominic with his "curse" thus sounds a note of irony, even bitter irony.

PLATE 19
Saint Dominic with the Crucifix (Cell 18)

THE SEVEN CELLS ALONG THE SOUTH CORRIDOR WERE RESERVED FOR
the use of the novices, and their classroom was the large cell at the
end. During their year of training, novices learned not only to adapt
themselves to the religious life of continuous prayer, fasting, and
other disciplines. They were also steeped in the history and customs
of the Dominican order. Novice masters in the Observance took special care to inculcate their charges with the relationship between
bodily action and inward disposition as regards prayer and meditation, something not unlike yoga.

This fresco shows Saint Dominic in one of the ways of prayer
that he was purported to have used and that were held up as a model
for the novices. Here, the arms crossed over his chest signify that he
has just completed a deep bow, which was thought to instill a sense
of humility at the beginning of prayer. One problem that the artist
faced, of course, is the fact that in all the frescoes of the novitiate
cells, Saint Dominic is shown kneeling. This made it impossible to
show the founder standing and bowing. But we know from the
prayer treatise called "The Nine Ways of Prayer" that he always
crossed his arms in this manner during his bow.

PLATE 20

Saint Dominic with the Crucifix (Cell 20)

IN THIS FRESCO, THE PAINTER SHOWED SAINT DOMINIC AS AN OLD man with a gray beard, unlike the beardless and more youthful version in Cell 18. In fact, Saint Dominic looks slightly different in each of the novices' cells, doubtless to underline the lifelong usefulness of the young novices' training. Here, Saint Dominic has shed his habit and, bare-chested, beats himself with the scourge. Although self-flagellation figured as the third way of prayer in the manual "The Nine Ways of Prayer," novices were forbidden to practice it alone. It did occur in communities of Observant Dominicans, but its use was confined to the whole group. The scourge might be applied during the daily Chapter of Faults in the case of a particular offense against the Rule or Constitutions. But more generally flagellation occurred at night during the last prayers of the day, called Compline. At that time, the whole community would expose their backs and a friar would pass among them with the scourge, hitting each one on the back in recognition of the repentance each friar was supposed to be feeling at that moment. The purpose of flagellation, as in all the manners of praying, was to underscore the relationship between the body and the mind. At this period, people believed that the body's appetites were one of the chief causes for mental or emotional disturbance. Curbing those appetites, therefore, meant increasing a sense of inner serenity.

PLATE 21

Saint Dominic with the Crucifix (Cell 21)

The figure of Saint Dominic in the fresco in Cell 21 recalls his gesture in the chapter room *Crucifixion*. In the sixth way of praying, Saint Dominic held his arms open, like a priest saying Mass. The text reads:

> Sometimes, as I was told personally by someone who had seen it, our holy father Dominic was also seen praying with his hands and arms spread out like a cross, stretching himself to the limit and standing as upright as he possibly could. . . . The holy man of God, Dominic, did not use this kind of prayer regularly, but only when, by God's inspiration, he knew that some great wonder was going to occur by virtue of his prayer. . . . When he raised the boy from the dead, praying standing with his arms and hands stretched out like a cross, we do not know what he said. . . . This makes it possible for any devout man of prayer to understand the teaching of this father, praying in this way when he desired to be extraordinarily moved towards God by the power of his prayer, or rather, when he felt himself being moved by God in a particularly expansive way, through some hidden inspiration, in view of some special grace for himself or for somebody else. ("The Nine Ways of Prayer," pp. 98–99)

PLATE 22
Virgin Mary with the Crucifix (Cell 22)

CELL 22 IS LOCATED AT THE END OF THE EAST CORRIDOR, ON THE RIGHT side. It is, therefore, the closest of the clerics' cells to the novices' dormitory. Furthermore, the fresco in this cell is unlike any of the other frescoes in the clerics' dormitory: It is rectangular rather than curved at the top; it has an alternating band of green and red in the frame rather than the gray moldings used in the clerics' cells; and its background is plain, white *intonaco*. Furthermore, the subject shows only one figure, in this case the Virgin Mary, seated beneath the Crucifix. In all these ways, therefore, the Cell 22 fresco resembles the novices' cell frescoes just examined and not the others on the east corridor where the clerics were housed. For these reasons, we may safely conclude that this cell was reserved for the use of the novice master. Although housed with the other clerics, he would, therefore, be close to the novices, and the position of his cell would enable him to monitor all comings and goings into the novices' dormitory. Furthermore, there is even better reason to believe that Cells 10 and 11, the two cells diagonally opposite, were the prior's cell and office.

PLATE 23

View into Cells 10 and 11

IN THE 1980S, CONSERVATORS DISCOVERED THAT CELLS 10 AND 11 had originally been joined by a large arch, since filled in. As the newly discovered double cell is unique at San Marco, it can have been only the prior's cell. And once one realized that fact, the subjects of the two frescoes became extremely relevant, as each was specially connected to the office and duties of the prior.

Priors were elected for a short term of about four years. Unlike monastic abbots, Dominican priors exercised limited authority and were subject to the continued endorsement of the chapter, as the electoral body of clerics was called. Beyond the local chapter, each convent belonged to a province whose boundaries were determined geographically; provincial chapters met regularly, attended by conventual priors and representatives elected by local chapters. The General Chapter of the whole order also met frequently—approximately every three years—and it, too, included voting members elected by the provinces. In these ways, the Dominicans were among the earliest truly democratic institutions within the Latin Church. Their system of governance by officers elected for limited terms, as well as their Constitutions, was widely imitated by later religious orders.

PLATE 24

Virgin and Child with Saints Dominic and Augustine (Cell 11)

ALTHOUGH THE AESTHETIC QUALITY OF THIS FRESCO ASSIGNS IT TO the hand of an assistant, its subject matter is relevant for understanding the other fresco in the double cell, which is one of Fra Angelico's masterpieces. This image is a kind of pictogram of the Dominican order. In his left hand the Christ Child holds the globe or orb that represents the whole world, exactly as on the San Marco altarpiece. The theme of Christ as the Universal Ruler is found frequently in Dominican art, by no means only at San Marco, and thus gives the fresco the resonance of Dominican universality. The attendant saints, too, are specifically apposite. Saint Augustine stands at the Virgin's right, the place of honor, and he holds an open book representing the Rule traditionally attributed to his authorship. It was adopted by a number of orders; but in this context, of course, the Rule of Saint Augustine is made specifically Dominican. Similarly, Saint Dominic holds an open book, which signifies the Constitutions, his unique contribution to the governance of religious life. In all these ways, the fresco, as well as the cell's location at the end of the east corridor, strongly suggests that Cell 11 was the prior's office.

PLATE 25

Presentation of Christ in the Temple (Cell 10)

IF CELL 11 WAS THE PRIOR'S OFFICE, THEN CELL 10 WAS HIS PRIVATE space. This exquisite fresco makes that even plainer. Like most of the frescoes in the clerics' cells, this one includes a Dominican saint— Peter Martyr, in this case—in one of the attitudes of prayer found in the manual that informed the subjects in the novices' cells. Saint Peter Martyr and the Prophetess Anna, on the far right, share the task of exemplifying the fourth way of Saint Dominic's praying, namely, alternately kneeling and standing. As the text of "The Nine Ways of Prayer" says: "Saint Dominic . . . look[ed] intently at Christ on the cross and [knelt] down over and over again, a hundred times perhaps. . . . And a great confidence would grow in our holy father Dominic, confidence in God's mercy for himself and . . . for the protection of the novices. . . ."

The scene itself shows the Presentation of Christ in the Temple (Luke 2:22–38). It had particular meaning for Dominican friars in general and for the friars of San Marco in particular. The feast itself, February 2, was solemnly observed in Dominican convents, with processions of lights in the cloister and church and with a solemn High Mass. This underscored the Dominicans' desire to imitate Christ's dedication to God in their own vocations. San Marco, furthermore, was home to a youth club dedicated to the Presentation. The friars closely supervised its activities, and the confraternity became a reliable source of recruits to the novitiate at San Marco.

PLATE 26

Presentation of Christ in the Temple (detail of Saint Simeon and the Christ Child)

THE PRESENTATION IS SOMETIMES CALLED "THE FEAST OF LIGHTS" because of the words recorded in Luke's gospel. According to the story, Mary and Joseph took the Infant Jesus to the Temple in Jerusalem in order to consecrate Jesus to God. When they handed the Child to Simeon the High Priest, Simeon recognized Jesus as the Christ. His song, known as the "Nunc dimittis," which was sung at San Marco every night before bed, calls the Child "a light for revelation to the Gentiles" (Luke: 2:29–32). Fra Angelico exploited both the text and the feast's traditional candlelight procession in the fresco. A strong light rakes across the surface as though it were falling through the open window just to the painting's right. In this detail, one can see how Fra Angelico used it to accentuate the quiet joy on the old man's face, and how that joy reflects—again, as light—into the Child's own beautiful and insouciant face as he gazes back at the high priest.

PLATE 27

Transfiguration (Cell 6)

THE TRANSFIGURATION (MATTHEW 17:1–8; MARK 9:2–8; LUKE 9:28–36) is the gospel reading for the last Sunday before Lent begins. As it foretells Christ's glory in the Resurrection, it is treated as a kind of liturgical bracket, along with Easter, between which the church meditates on the Lord's Passion and Death. Fra Angelico clearly intended the friar in Cell 6 to make the association between the Transfiguration and the Crucifixion, because he shows Christ with this arms extended as though on the Cross, a feature that, so far as we know, is original with Fra Angelico. Furthermore, the texts all accentuate the story's nighttime setting, the miraculous appearance of Moses and Elijah (here indicated only by their heads), and most of all, the brilliant radiance that burst from Christ himself. For these reasons we may also imagine that the subject had special appeal for Fra Angelico, because it gave him yet another opportunity, as the *Presentation* had done, to experiment with various luminescent effects. It is worth noticing, for example, that the faces of Saint Dominic and the Virgin Mary, who do not figure in the biblical narrative, are lit from "outside" the picture, whereas the three apostles in the foreground are bathed in the aura that emanates from the figure of Christ.

PLATE 28

Transfiguration (detail of the head of Christ)

As no documents concerning the building and decorating of San Marco have ever come to light, we cannot know precisely when Fra Angelico and his assistants painted the frescoes. But the frescoes themselves allow us to know how many working sessions (*giornate*) each one took, because the slight ridges separating the *giornate* make it possible to count them. Furthermore, we also know that fresco painters worked from the top down, and it is therefore also possible to retrace the exact sequence in which each painting was made. Most of the cell frescoes are made up of four or five *giornate*, but the *Transfiguration*, alone, required eight. Fra Angelico devoted one entire *giornata* to this life-size face of Christ, underscoring the importance in which he held this image. Indeed, the face of Christ has always challenged artists; Leonardo da Vinci, for example, put off painting Christ's face in the *Last Supper* until the very end. Fra Angelico, obviously eager that this image be exactly as he wished it, applied the paint in small, deliberate strokes and frequently shifted hues and values, as though it were a painting in tempera, using the light to endow the head with an almost sculptural sense of three-dimensional solidity. This is the most solemn and majestic head of Christ in all of Fra Angelico's work and must be regarded as his definitive statement, as it were, of the most sacred theme in Christian art.

PLATE 29
Coronation of the Virgin (Cell 9)

THE *Coronation of the Virgin* AS QUEEN OF HEAVEN IS THE ONLY fresco in the dormitory of San Marco that is not based on a biblical passage. Here it almost certainly marks the feasts of August 15, the Assumption of the Virgin, and of November 1, All Saints. The three Dominican saints, plus Saints Benedict, Francis, and Mark, kneel in a semicircle below the image of Christ and his Mother. The Coronation itself happens in an explosion of light that to modern eyes recalls a starry nebula or supernova, seeming constantly to expand from a white-hot core of unapproachable brilliance at the center, between the two figures. As in the *Presentation* and the *Transfiguration*, Fra Angelico exploited both the white pigments and the intonaco support, along with a peachy glow, like sunlight, behind the saintly figures below. The entire composition is visionary. The saints are suspended in heaven itself, on clouds; they do not look directly at the Coronation. Instead, one can imagine that what they "see" is in their mind's, not their body's, eyes, and that the viewer, like the saints, is somehow privy to an occurrence so transcendent that its representation is lifted above the plane of reality, where heavy, corporeal bodies must be shown responding to the pull of gravity and interrupting the fall of light. In this fresco neither Christ nor the Virgin is subject to such limitations of the flesh.

PLATE 30
Mocking of Christ (Cell 7)

THIS IMAGE IS DERIVED FROM THE PASSION ACCOUNT OF CHRIST'S being crowned with thorns and mocked by Pilate's soldiers, just prior to the Crucifixion (Matthew 27:27–31; Mark, 15:16–20; John 19:1–3). Christ, shown almost twice as large as the figures of the Virgin Mary and Saint Dominic in the foreground, sits on a bench, wearing a white robe and carrying a bamboo stick in one hand and what looks like a stone or a sponge in the other, ironic symbols of kingship, but also instruments of torture. Hands and a strangely bodiless head, spitting, behind Christ increase the painting's mystery and ambiguity. This is the fresco that first-time visitors to San Marco remember most when they leave. Few fail to remark on the fresco's atmosphere of emptiness and sadness; each of the figures seems isolated in his or her own particular grief. Both the Virgin Mary and Saint Dominic hold one hand on their chin. From "The Nine Ways of Prayer" we know that this signifies devout reading, and, indeed, Saint Dominic holds an open book on his lap, doubtless intended to be opened to one of the gospel passages cited above. When one realizes, then, that the fresco is intended to prompt an act of *meditation*, that it does not "tell a story," the oddly unreal aspects in the background seem less important as narrative details and more important as subjects for pondering.

PLATE 31

Mocking of Christ (detail of Christ's head)

IF IT IS CORRECT TO HYPOTHESIZE THAT FRA ANGELICO WORKED FROM south to north in the clerics' dormitory, beginning with the prior's Cell 10, he painted this face of Christ before he faced a similar task in the Cell 6 *Transfiguration*. Indeed, the resemblance between these two faces is strong, stronger than between either one and the faces of Christ in the cloister frescoes. Could it be that Fra Angelico intended this comparison? After all, the frescoes are in adjoining cells, only a few feet apart. In the *Transfiguration*, Fra Angelico lavished attention on the details of Christ's serene, majestic face. Here, many of those details are hidden behind the blindfold around Christ's head. But in a tour-de-force of fresco painting, which is usually a highly opaque medium, Fra Angelico painted the white blindfold as translucent, thus allowing the beholder to see Christ's eyes, now closed in suffering and humiliation, which in the *Transfiguration* fresco shone with the numinous power of the Godhead. Furthermore, Fra Angelico counterposes Christ's refined features against the coarse, even ugly, face of the tormentor spitting at him, using not only contrast but irony to draw one's attention ever more intently to the visage of the suffering Savior.

PLATE 32
Annunciation (Cell 3)

As elsewhere at San Marco, here Fra Angelico used technique to communicate his interpretation of the subject. The scene is drenched in light, expressed not as the complex system of shadows deployed in the *Annunciation* in the north corridor, but as veils of transparent washes spread over the white surfaces of the cloister—again, the fresco's setting is derived from the actual building in which it appears. Moreover, the Virgin Mary's gown is, technically speaking, unfinished. It is painted in thin layers of red earth, which is the traditional preparation in fresco technique for a final layer of blue. But Fra Angelico omitted the final layer altogether and left only the underpainting.

These devices take on special meaning in light of the painting's central message, which is found in the figure of Saint Peter Martyr standing at the left edge, his hands joined at the palms. According to "The Nine Ways of Prayer," this gesture inspired humility. Furthermore, this is one of only a handful of representations of the Annunciation in which the Virgin's head is lower than the angel's. In the medieval and Renaissance pictorial language of rank, the higher the personage, the higher his or her head in a painting. Fra Angelico thus inverted that rule as a further sign of the Virgin's humility. And that—the friar's desire to seek humility—is the primary message of this fresco.

PLATE 33
Noli Me Tangere (Cell 1)

ACCORDING TO MATTHEW, MARK, AND LUKE, MARY MAGDALENE was among the women who first witnessed Christ's Resurrection. John's gospel, however, places Mary Magdalene alone in the garden and tells how she mistook the Risen Christ for a gardener (John 20:1–2, 11–18). When she did recognize him, she reached out to him, saying, "Rabbouni." "Do not touch me," Christ said in response—in the Vulgate—"*Noli me tangere.*" And that is how the subject gets its name.

Among the frescoes in the clerics' cells, this one is anomalous in two important respects. First, it is the only fresco that actually tells a story. The artist shows Mary Magdalene kneeling and reaching out toward Christ, who has the gardener's hoe over his left shoulder; he steps away so quickly that his right foot crosses over the left. All the other frescoes communicate messages *about* a biblical narrative, but they do not actually show the episode in progress. Second, all but one of the other frescoes depicts a saint posed in one of Saint Dominic's nine ways of praying; in this way, the friar-beholder was encouraged to imitate the founder's process of meditating on scriptural texts. The other exception is the novice master's Cell 22, which shows only the Virgin Mary. As its composition resembles those in the novices' cells, and as the *Noli Me Tangere* bears many similarities with the frescoes in the cells on the north corridor, we may deduce that Cell 1, at the beginning of the east corridor, housed the friar charged with overseeing the lay brothers.

PLATE 34

Crucifixion (Cell 37)

A REDUCED AND SIMPLIFIED VERSION OF THE *Crucifixion* IN THE chapter room, the fresco in Cell 37 is one of the largest in the dormitory. Furthermore, the cell itself is among the most spacious; and its location corresponds with the novices' meeting room at the end of the south corridor. The resemblance to the chapter room fresco, the room's size, and its location at the end of the corridor are all features that lead one to conclude that this was the room where the lay brothers gathered for their meetings with their master. The Dominican standing at the foot of the Cross may be recognized as Saint Dominic by the little red star in his halo. But no symbol identifies the friar kneeling at the right, although his halo and corpulence suggest that he is Saint Thomas Aquinas, whom one would naturally expect to find in a Dominican classroom.

Plate 35
Communion of the Apostles (Cell 35)

This scene is clearly based on the Last Supper, but there are interesting and important differences. Most obvious is the fact that Christ is shown giving Communion to the apostles, who are seated at a table and in a room obviously designed to recall the refectory at San Marco. Even a wellhead, which may originally have stood in the center of the cloister, is shown through the open door on the right.

The *Communion of the Apostles* symbolizes the Feast of Corpus Christi, a celebration in honor of Christ's presence in the bread and wine of the Mass, which was a major feature of the Dominican liturgical year. In his *Summa theologiae*, Saint Thomas Aquinas had defined that presence in the philosophical construction known as transubstantiation, and he was credited with having written the Corpus Christi hymn and office, which Dominican communities celebrated with special dignity. Through this image, then, a lay brother was reminded that Christ himself served at table, just as lay brothers at San Marco did, and that each of the community's meals could be understood as a "communion" with the Lord. Indeed, a fresco of Christ as the Man of Sorrows, a common Eucharistic symbol, appeared over the entrance into the refectory from the cloister.

PLATE 36
Agony in the Garden (Cell 34)

LIKE THE LAST SUPPER (AT SAN MARCO THE *Communion of the Apostles*), the Agony in the Garden is another scene almost always found in Passion cycles. But like the fresco in Cell 35, which interpreted the Last Supper in ways specially appropriate to Dominicans, this *Agony in the Garden* departs from tradition in interesting ways. In the background one sees Christ, kneeling and receiving the chalice from an angel (Matthew 26:42) while the apostles Peter, James, and John sleep in the middle ground. These are all common features of the subject. The unusual feature is the appearance of Mary and Martha, identified on their halos, crouched in a strange interior in the foreground. Their presence may be explained by the significance of these two women for lay brothers. Sisters of Jesus' friend Lazarus, whom Christ raised from the dead (John 11:1–44), Mary and Martha have always been the patron saints of housekeepers. Although they do not appear in any of the accounts of the Passion, Fra Angelico, who probably designed but did not paint this fresco, included them here in order to relate the mysteries of Christ's death and Resurrection to those of the lay brothers who were cooks, housekeepers, and sacristans at San Marco.

PLATE 37

Sermon on the Mount (Cell 32)

NOT ALL THE CELLS IN A DOMINICAN DORMITORY WERE BEDROOMS. Some were storage rooms; some, like Cell 37, were meeting rooms; some, like Cell 11, were offices. Others, as we have seen, were classrooms, and a classroom is probably what Cell 32 was originally. The *Sermon on the Mount* is not part of the Passion cycle; its subject points to Christ as *teacher*. Furthermore, Cell 32's large size and location just across the corridor from the library suggest that it was where the lector worked. After the prior, the lector was the most important officer in a Dominican convent. His title comes from the Latin word meaning "reader," and this reflects the lector's duties of giving theological lectures and overseeing the friars' various courses of study. As an Order of Preachers, the Dominicans were particularly pledged to intellectual work; although the Observants discouraged learning for its own sake, they, like the conventual friars, were careful to assure the theological orthodoxy of their sermons. Lectors, therefore, were as active in Observant convents as in conventual ones. As the lector, like the prior, was allowed two cells, and as the only truly double cell are known as 10 and 11, we may suppose that Cell 32 was the lector's study and office. There is no way to determine which of the clerics' cells he was intended to occupy. As its particular location is unimportant—unlike the prior's, lay brother master's, and novice master's—the lector could have been privately housed in any cell along the east corridor.

PLATE 38

Jesus Consigning His Mother to Saint John (Cell 38)

COSIMO DE' MEDICI ENJOYED THE SINGULAR PRIVILEGE OF HAVING his own double cell at the end of the north corridor at San Marco. Originally, it probably opened onto a terrace that stretched across the north side of the dormitory and led to the library. (This feature of the dormitory had already disappeared with additions to the building in the sixteenth century.) Thus, Cosimo could use his cell for prayer and study and visit his library without having to disturb the friars by using the interior corridor. This fresco, high up on the wall, is now above a window made from walling up the door leading onto the terrace. It shows four saints kneeling below the Cross. Left to right, they are Saint Cosmas, the Virgin Mary, Saint John the Evangelist, and Saint Peter Martyr. To the right of Christ's body appear the words with which Jesus consigned his mother to Saint John's care (John 19:26–27). The male saints, of course, are Medici patrons—Cosmas for Cosimo, John for Cosimo's father Giovanni, and Peter Martyr for Cosimo's son Piero—just as in the chapter room *Crucifixion*, the *Madonna of the Shadows*, and most important, the San Marco altarpiece. In this way, Fra Angelico was able to weld the Passion theme that unites all the cell frescoes on the north corridor to Cosimo's own personal interests.

PLATE 39
Adoration of the Magi (Cell 39)

THE *Adoration of the Magi* ADORNS THE SEMICIRCULAR WALL OF THE inner of Cosimo's two adjoining cells. In the center at the bottom is a niche in which is painted the *Man of Sorrows* with instruments of the Passion at the sides; there is a hole in the floor of this niche. The combination of the major scene with this little niche indicates beyond doubt that this was Cosimo's private chapel, as the niche must have contained the Sacrament, which we know the pope had entitled Cosimo to keep. The scene showing the Three Magi adoring the Christ Child is incoherent in terms of the other frescoes in this part of the dormitory; but the Magi, after all, were other patrons of the Medici. Indeed, the annual Magi Procession of January 6, which started at the cathedral and terminated at San Marco, was an occasion when Medici power was most in evidence, and the painting in Cosimo's private chapel at San Marco signals the peculiar mix of politics and religion so common in Florentine life of this period.

The artist was almost certainly Fra Angelico's trusted assistant, Benozzo Gozzoli. After Fra Angelico's death in 1455, Benozzo became a successful and respected painter in his own right. His masterpiece, in fact, is a later version of precisely this fresco; he painted the great Magi Procession on the walls of the chapel in the Medici Palace, which Cosimo began to build shortly after San Marco was dedicated in 1443 (see fig. 6).

PLATE 40

Piercing of Christ's Side (Cell 42)

IN THE SEQUENCE OF MOSTLY BANAL *Crucifixions* IN THE CELLS between Cosimo's cells and the library, almost certainly reserved for guests, there is one of very great beauty. It shows the *Piercing of Christ's Side*, with Saint Dominic kneeling in the foreground. Saints Mary and Martha appear again, as in Cell 34, but their averted faces—we do not even seen Saint Martha's—and eloquent gestures are full of a quiet pathos that cannot fail to move the beholder. The generous intervals between the figures, the masterful handling of gestures and draperies, and most of all, its high, elegiac tone point to Fra Angelico as the author. This is the only fresco actually by his hand in the cells on the north corridor, and it comes from very late in his career, certainly in the 1450s. It was, in fact, probably the last painting Fra Angelico made at San Marco before leaving for Rome, where he died.

Glossary

Affresco   (from the word for "fresh"; in English, "fresco"). Painting on freshly laid plaster with pigments dissolved in water. As plaster and paint dry together, they become united chemically. Known as "true" fresco (or "buon fresco"), but frequently used in combination with "secco" (see below) details, this technique was in general use for mural painting in Italy from the late thirteenth century on.

Arriccio   (literally, "rough"). The first layer of plaster spread on the masonry in preparation for painting; the "sinopia" (see below) is executed on this surface. It was purposely left rough so that the top layer (see "intonaco") would adhere to it more firmly.

Cartone   (from the word for "heavy paper"; in English, "cartoon"). An enlarged version of the main lines of the final composition done on paper or cloth, sometimes, but not always, equal in size to the area to be painted. The cartoon was used to transfer the design to the wall; it could be divided into several sections for the creation of one large image. The cartoon was laid against the wall over the final layer of fresh plaster, so that outlines of the forms could be either incised with a stylus or transferred by "pouncing" (see "spolvero"). In either case, the outlines were used as guides for the artist to paint. The procedure was in common use by the second half of the fifteenth century although it had been developed earlier.

Giornata   (from the word for "day"). The patch of "intonaco" to be painted "daily," not necessarily in one day. The artist decided in advance the size of the surface he would paint and laid on top of the "arriccio" or rough plaster only the amount of fresh "intonaco" or fine plaster needed for his work. The joinings usually are discernible upon a close examination of the painted surface, and they disclose the order in which the patches were painted because each successive patch slightly overlaps the preceding one.

Intonaco   (literally "whitewash," or fine plaster). The final smooth layer of plaster on which painting with colors was carried out. Made from lime, fine sand, and marble dust and laid in sections (see "giornata").

Pounce, pouncing   Fine powder, usually pulverized charcoal, dusted over a stencil to transfer a design to an underlying surface.

Secco   (literally "dry"). Painting on plaster that has already dried. The colors are mixed with an adhesive or binder to attach the color to the surface to be painted. The binding medium may be made from various substances, such as tempera. "Tempera" (pigment and animal or vegetable glue) or less often "tempera grassa" (pigment and egg) was commonly used to complete a composition already painted in fresco. Because the pigment and the dry wall surface do not become thoroughly united, as they do in true fresco, mural paintings done in tempera (or "a secco") tend to deteriorate and flake off the walls more rapidly.

Sinopia   Originally a red ochre named after Sinope, a town on the Black Sea that was well known for its red pigments. In fresco technique the term was used for the final preparatory drawing on the "arriccio," which was normally executed in red ochre.

Spolvero   (from the word for "dust"). An early method (see "cartone") of transferring the artist's drawings onto the "intonaco." After drawings as large as the frescoes were made on paper, their outlines were pricked, and the paper was cut into pieces the size of each day's work. After the day's patch of "intonaco" was laid, the corresponding drawing was placed over it and "dusted" with a cloth sack filled with charcoal powder, some of which passed through the tiny punctured holes to mark the design on the fresh "intonaco."

Annotated Bibliography

Baxandall, Michael. *Painting and Experience in Fifteenth-Century Italy*. Oxford: Clarendon Press, 1972. A provocative set of observations on how paintings in the early Renaissance were actually perceived; specially useful for religious art.

Borsook, Eve. *The Mural Painters of Tuscany*. 2d ed. Oxford: Oxford University Press, 1980. The definitive study of the techniques, styles, and other issues of fresco painting.

Brucker, Gene. *Renaissance Florence*. Berkeley: University of California Press [1983], ©1969. An excellent, readable, and highly informative introduction to the culture of Renaissance Florence.

Gilbert, Creighton. "The Conversion of Fra Angelico." In *Scritti di Storia dell'Arte in onore di Roberto Salvini*, ed. C. De Benedictis, Florence: G.C. Sansoni Editore Nuova, 1984, pp. 281–87. A masterful interpretation of documents long known, which reconstructs an entirely convincing set of circumstances that can account for Fra Angelico's entrance into the Order of Preachers at a rather advanced age.

Hay, Dennis. *The Church in Italy in the Fifteenth Century*. Cambridge: Cambridge University Press, 1977. A short, readable overview of the institutional and doctrinal issues, providing a wider context for understanding the Dominican Observance.

Hinnebusch, William, O.P. *The History of the Dominican Order*. 2 vols., New York: Alba House, 1965 and 1973. The standard account in English.

Hood, William. *Fra Angelico at San Marco*. New Haven and London: Yale University Press, 1993. The only book-length treatment of Fra Angelico's work for San Marco, it also studies Renaissance monastic decoration in general.

Kent, Dale. *The Rise of the Medici. Faction in Florence 1426–1434*. Oxford: Oxford University Press, 1978. A careful and fascinating account of the Medici rise to power.

Painting and Illumination in Early Renaissance Florence 1300–1450, ed. Laurence B. Kanter et al. Exhibition catalogue. New York: The Metropolitan Museum of Art, 1994. A recent exhibition, with a superb scholarly catalogue containing essays by noted experts, that brought together exactly the kinds of paintings and painters out of which Fra Angelico's early career grew.

Pope-Hennessy, John. *Fra Angelico*. 2d ed. London: Phaidon, 1974. Still the most reliable monograph with catalogue raisonné.

Strehlke, Carl Brandon. "Fra Angelico Studies." In *Painting and Illumination in Early Renaissance Florence 1300–1450*, ed. Laurence B. Kanter et al., Exhibition catalogue. New York: The Metropolitan Museum of Art, 1994, pp. 25–43. The most recent contribution to Fra Angelico studies, with bold theses about the artist's beginnings, it supplements material found in Hood 1993.

"The Nine Ways of Prayer" [of Saint Dominic], trans. S. Tugwell, in *Early Dominicans. Selected Writings*, ed. Simon Tugwell, O.P., New York, Ramsey and Toronto: Paulist Press, 1982, pp. 94–103. *De Modo Orandi*, the thirteenth-century prayer manual purporting to have been composed by a friar in the convent at Bologna, who spied on Saint Dominic while he was alone in prayer, and recorded the saint's actions.

Vasari, Giorgio. *The Lives of the Artists, a Selection*. trans. G. Bull, New York: Penguin Books, 1965. An abbreviated, but highly readable, one-volume version of the *Lives*, but containing the biography of Fra Angelico.

LIST OF BLACK-AND-WHITE FIGURES

LIST OF COLOR PLATES